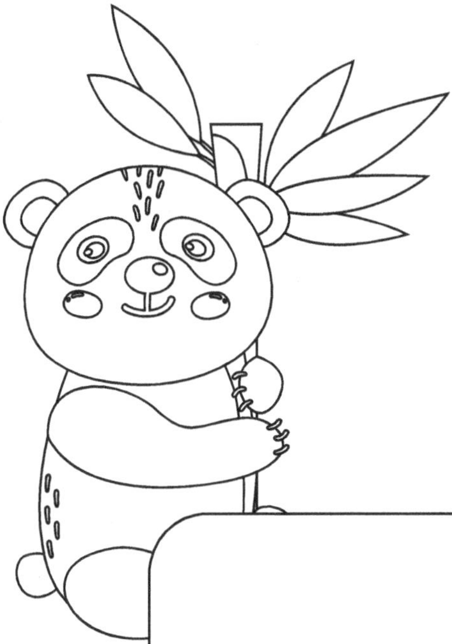

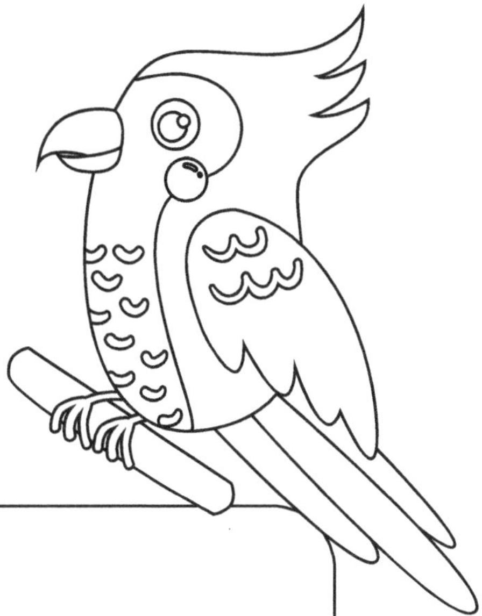

This Book Belongs To:

____

____

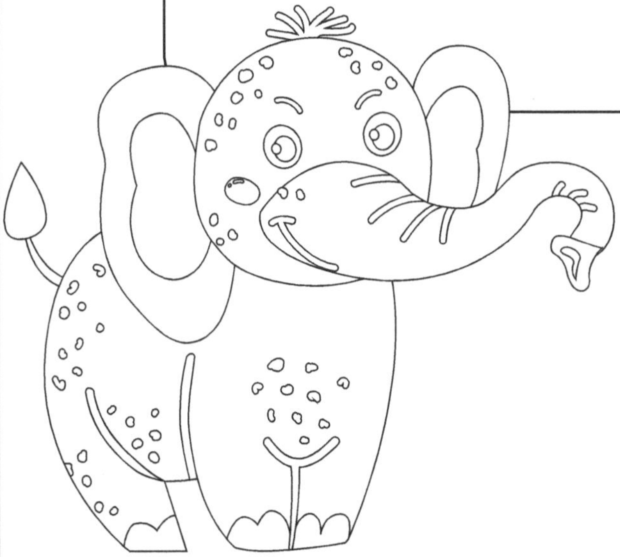

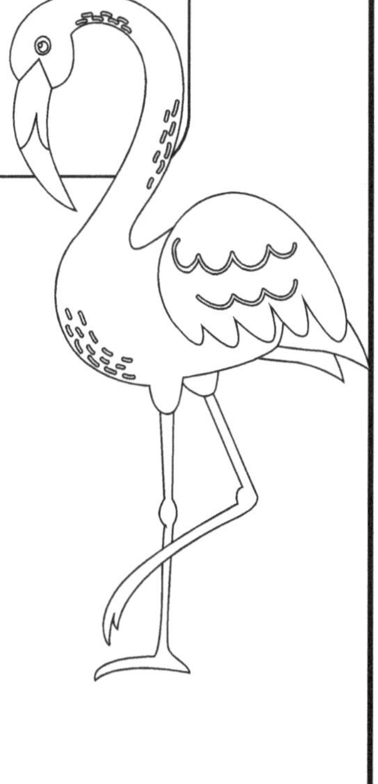

Farm Animals

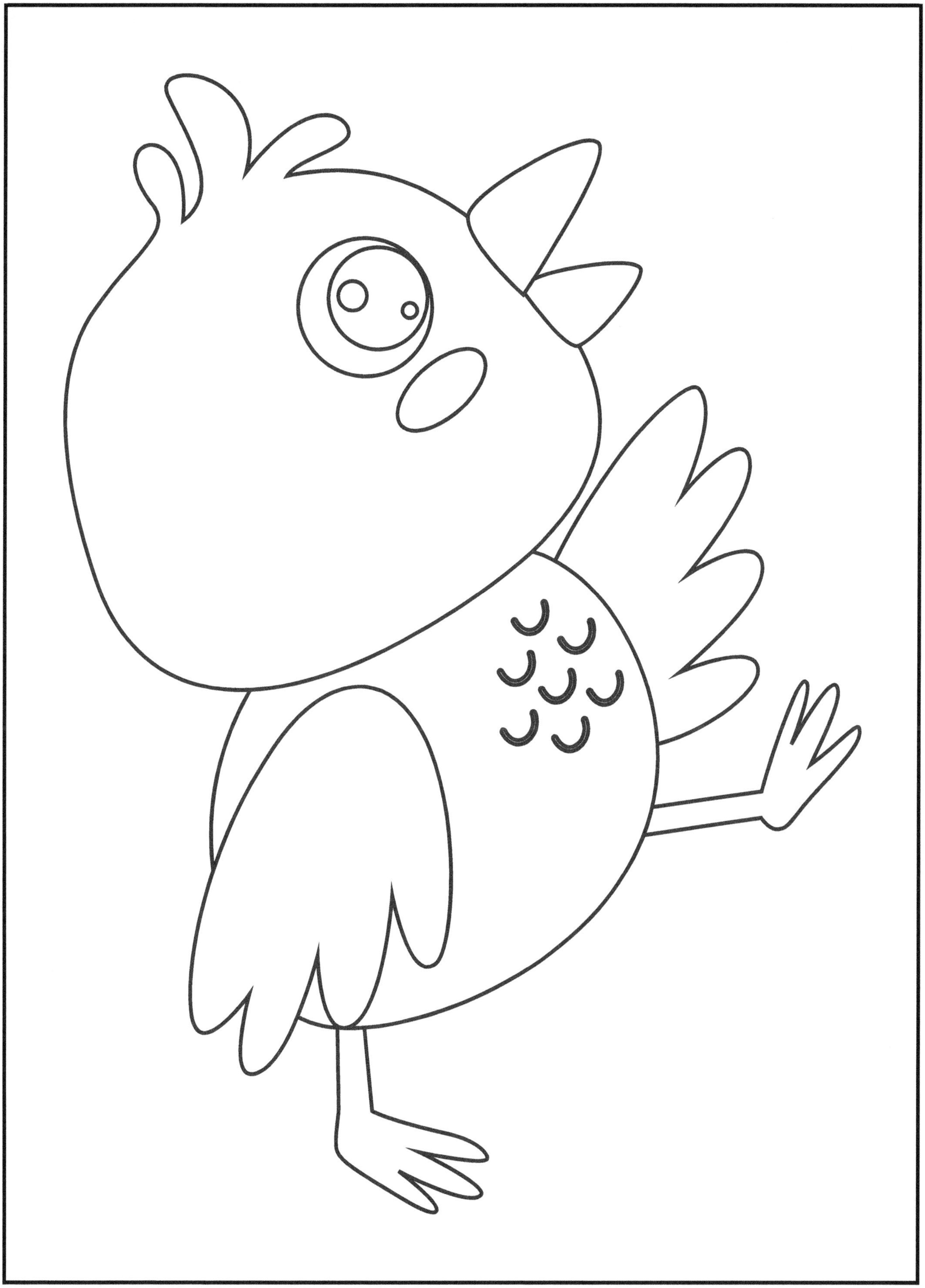

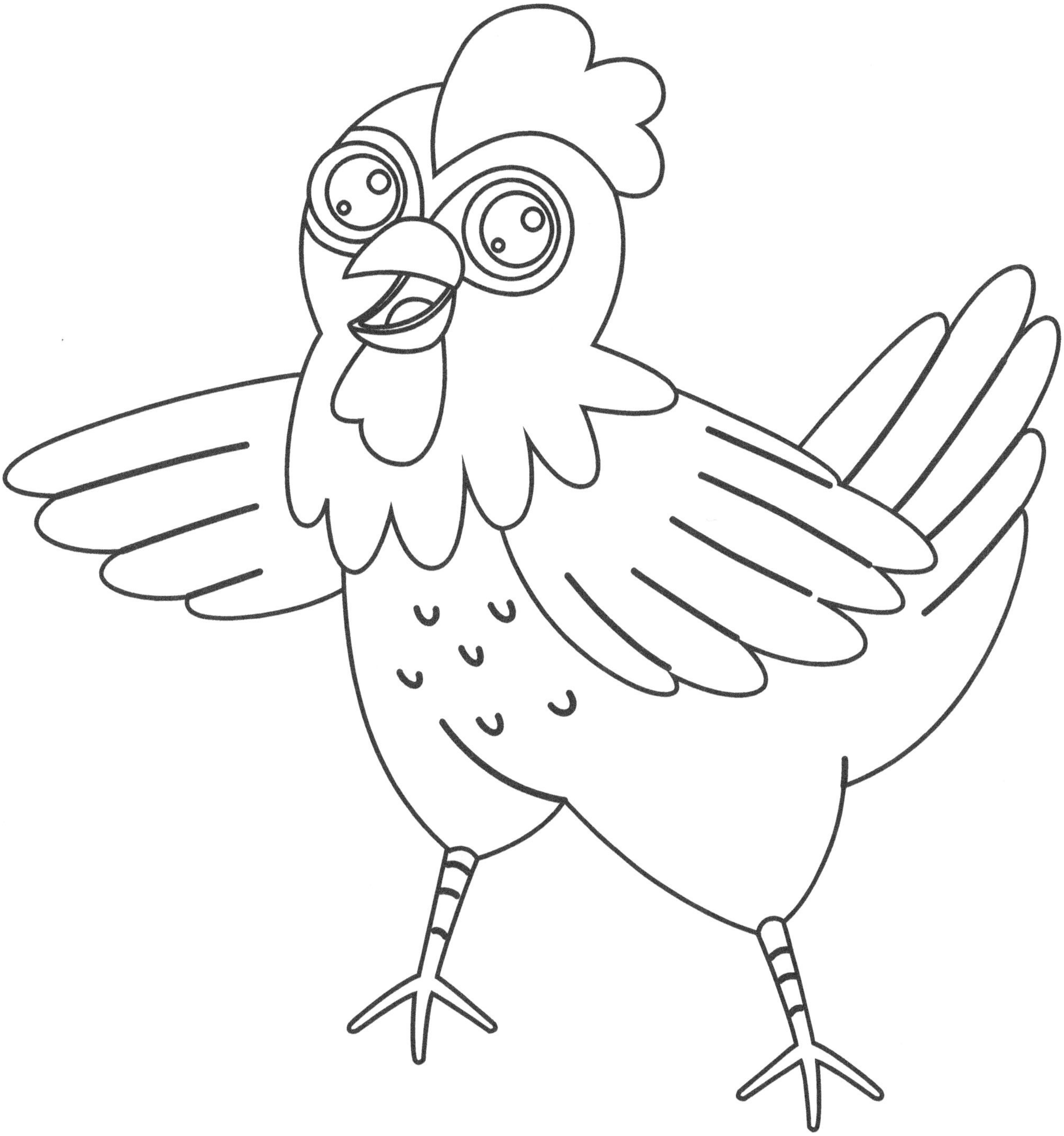

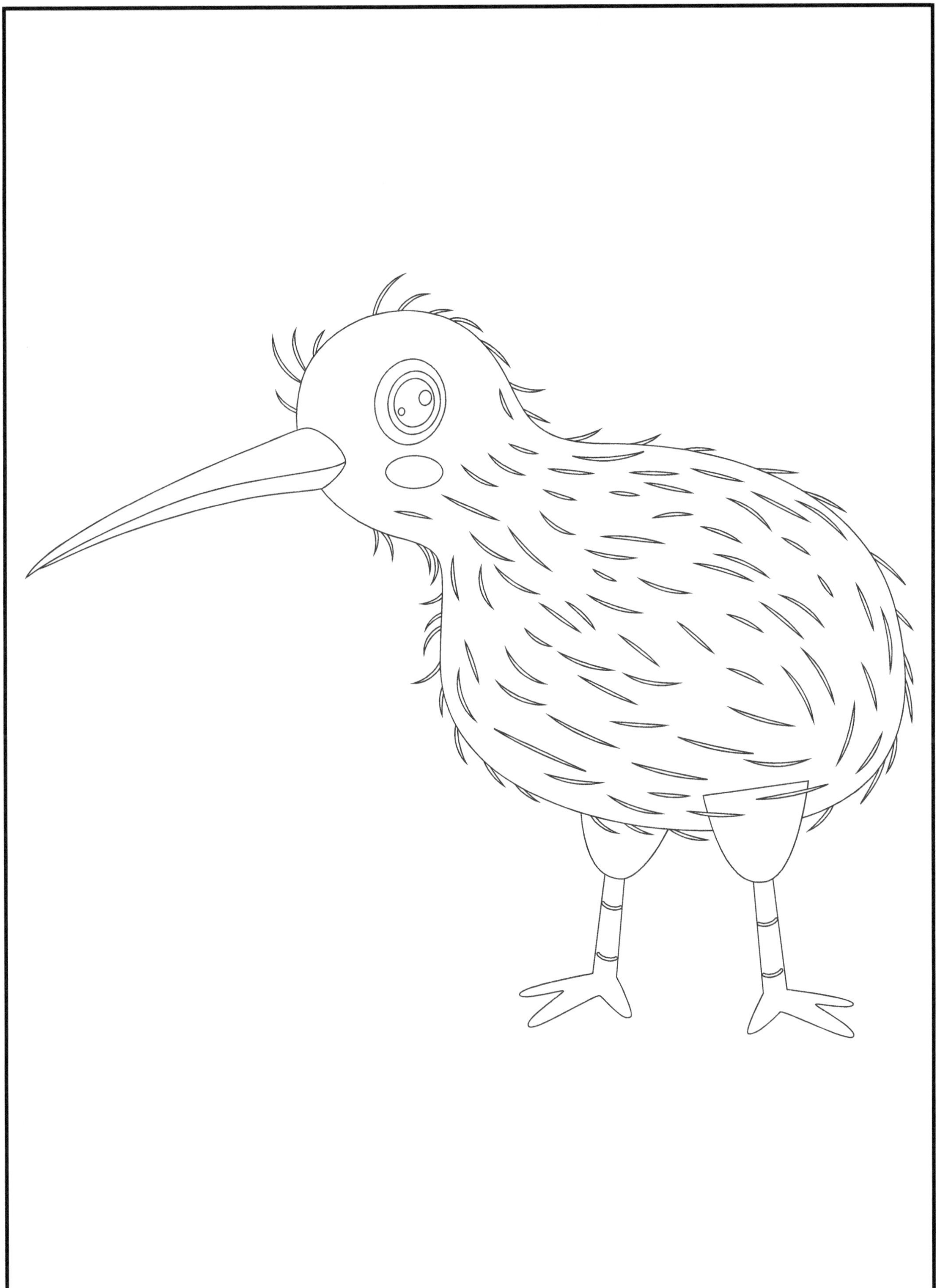

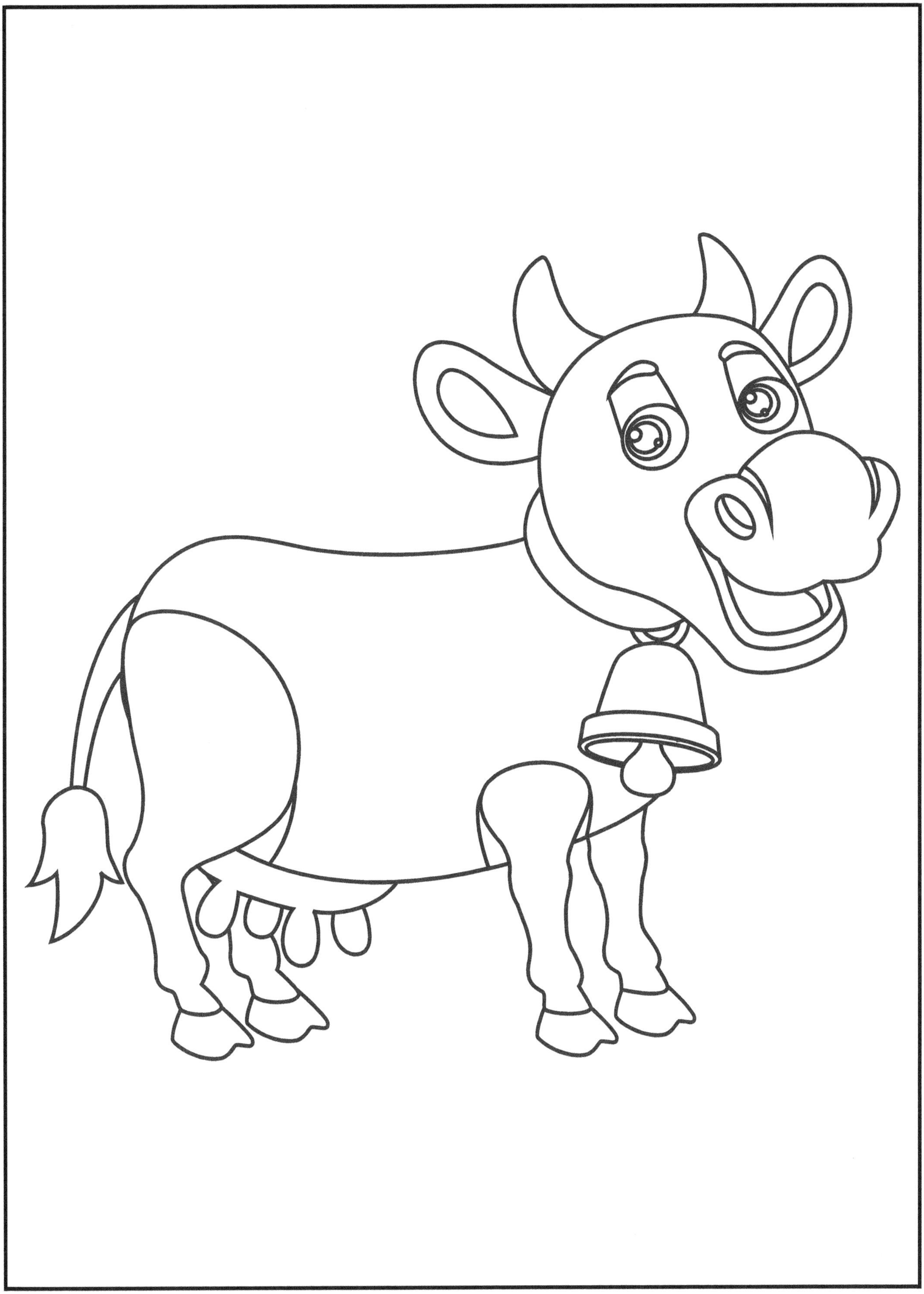

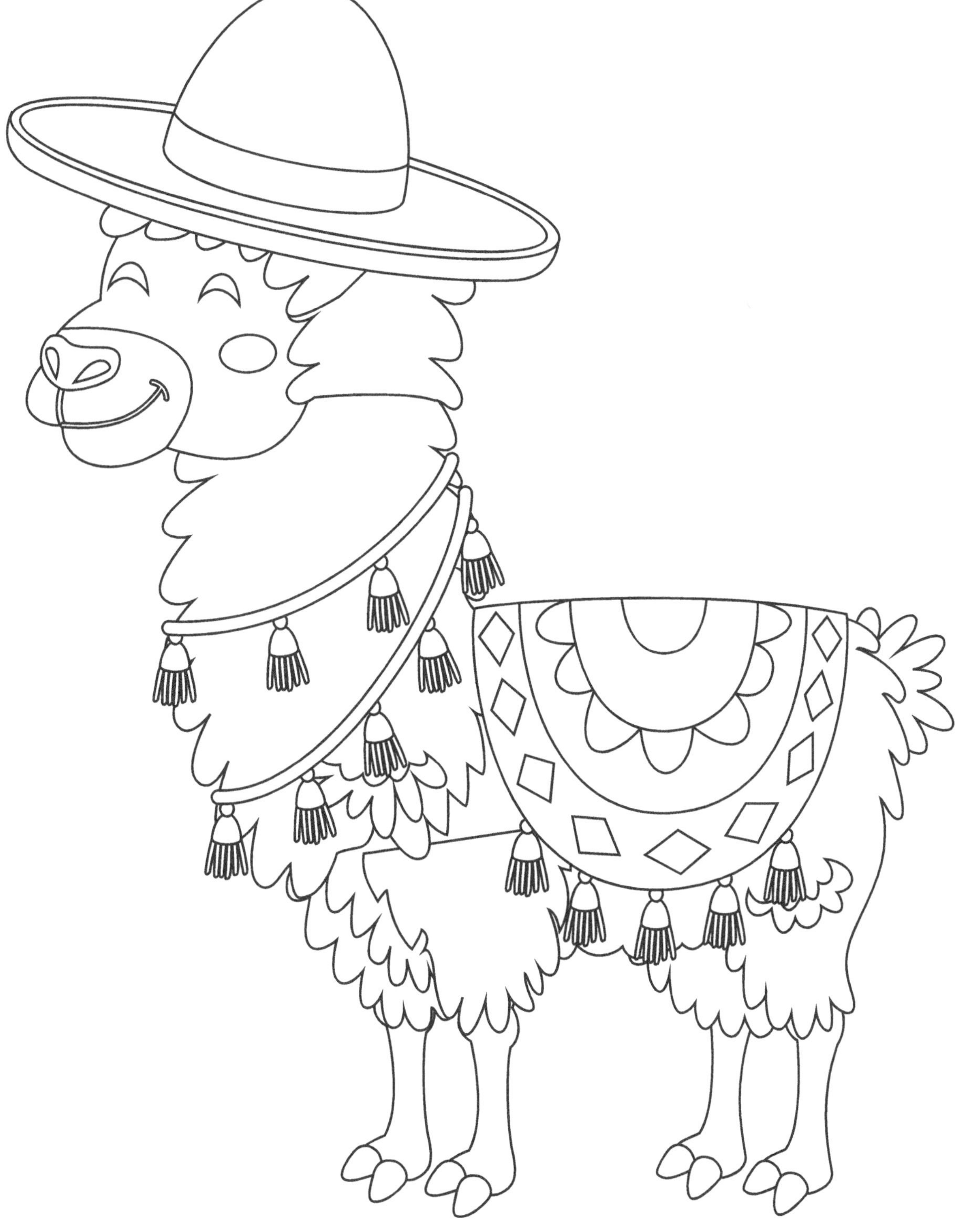

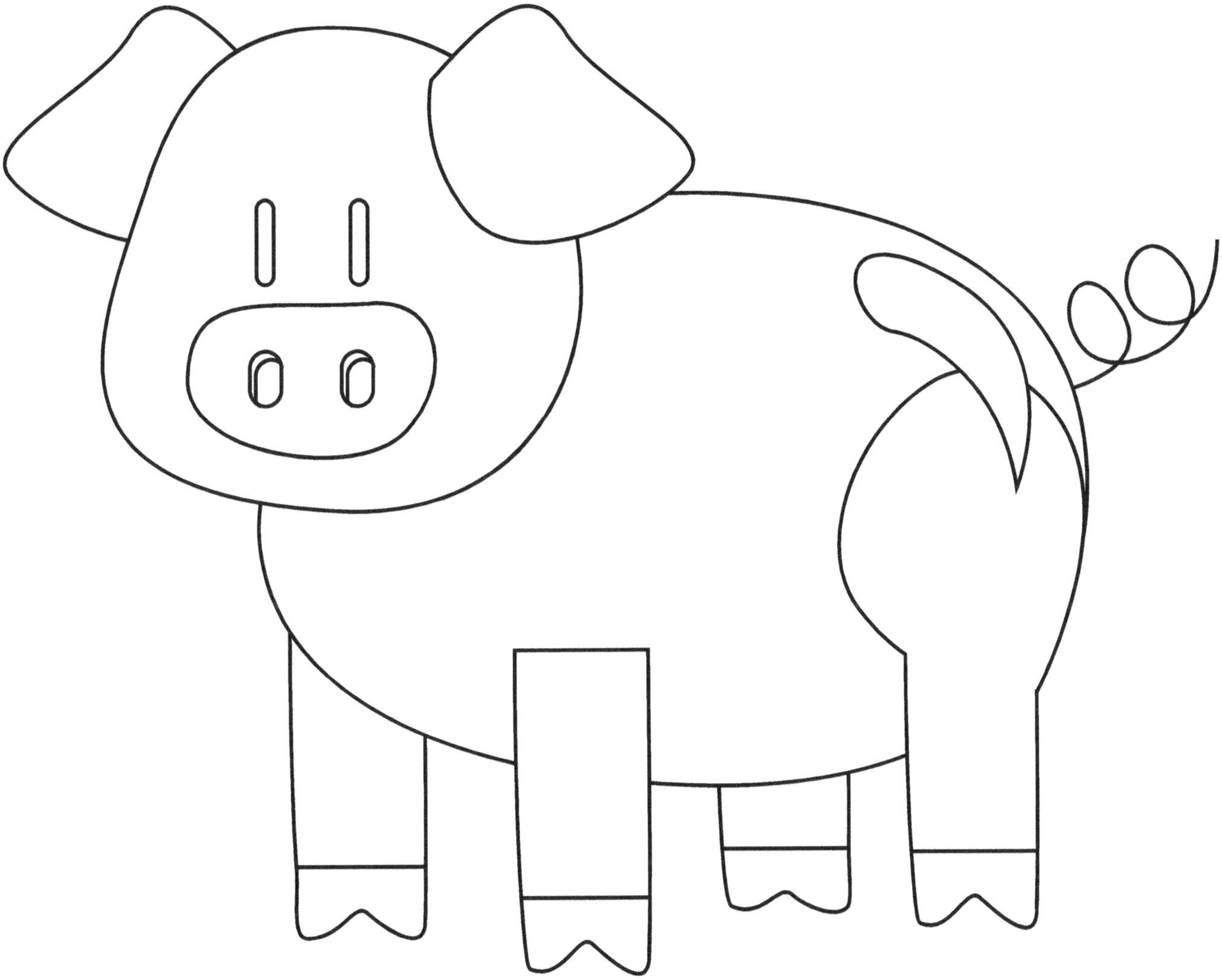

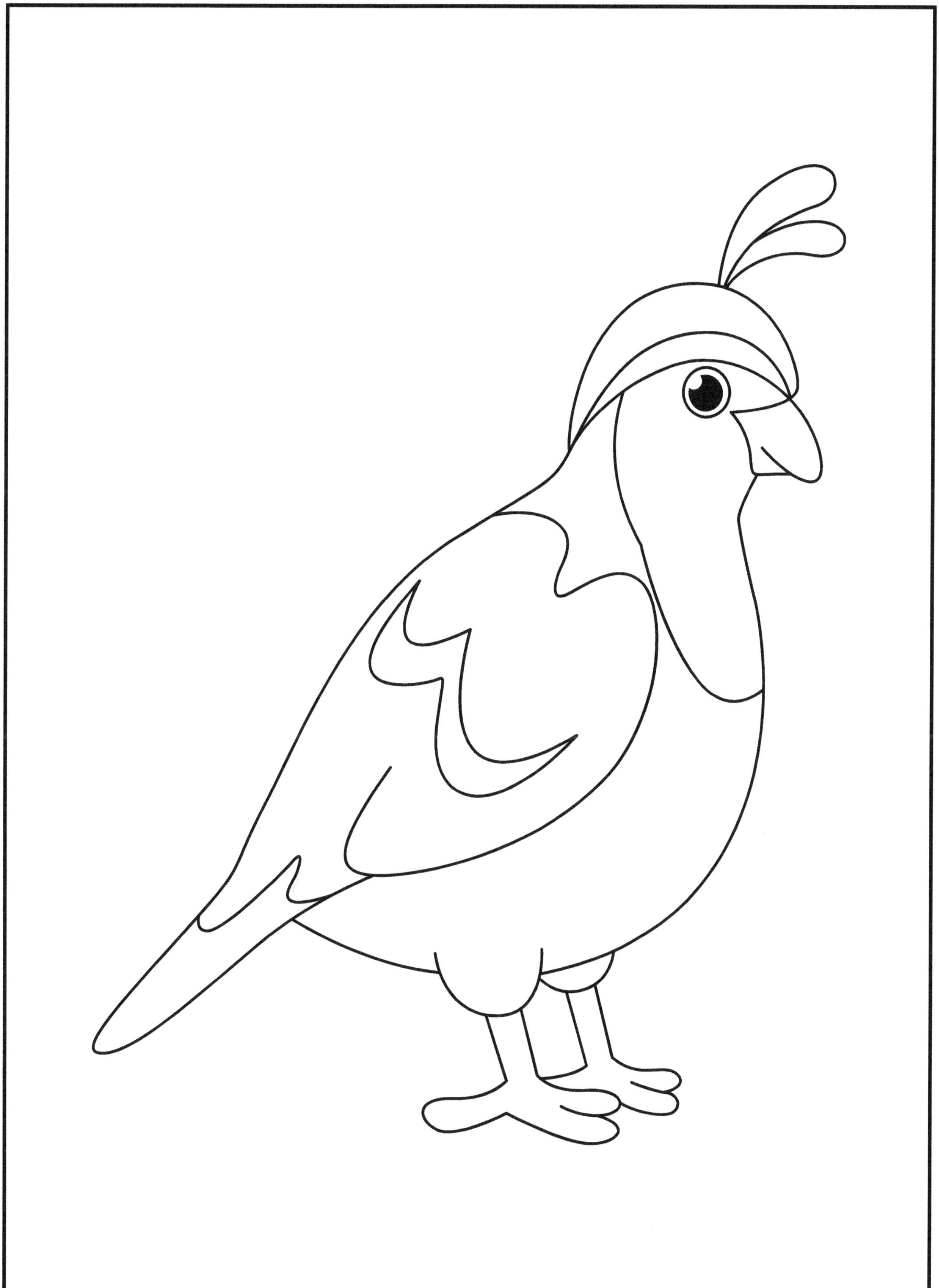

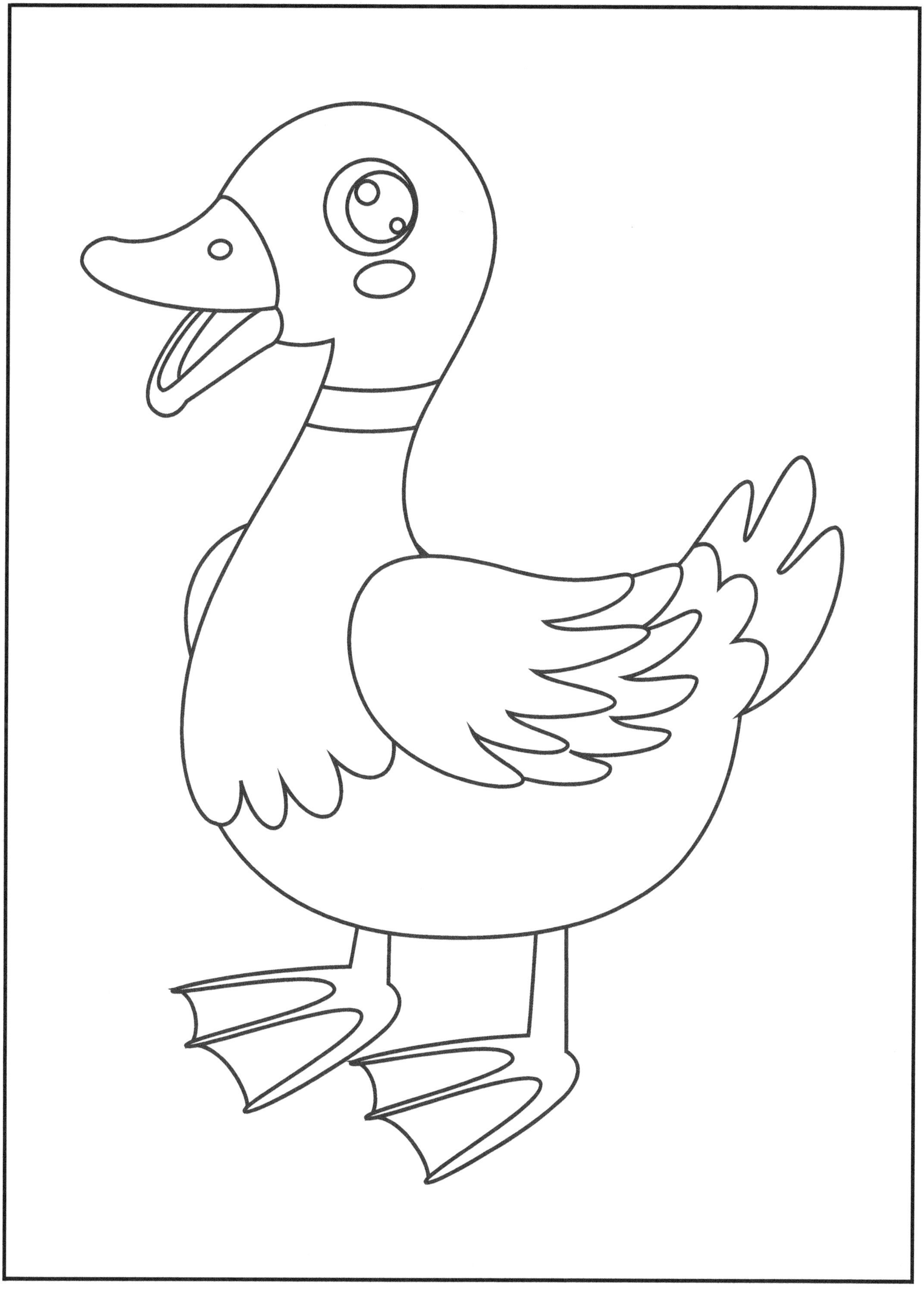

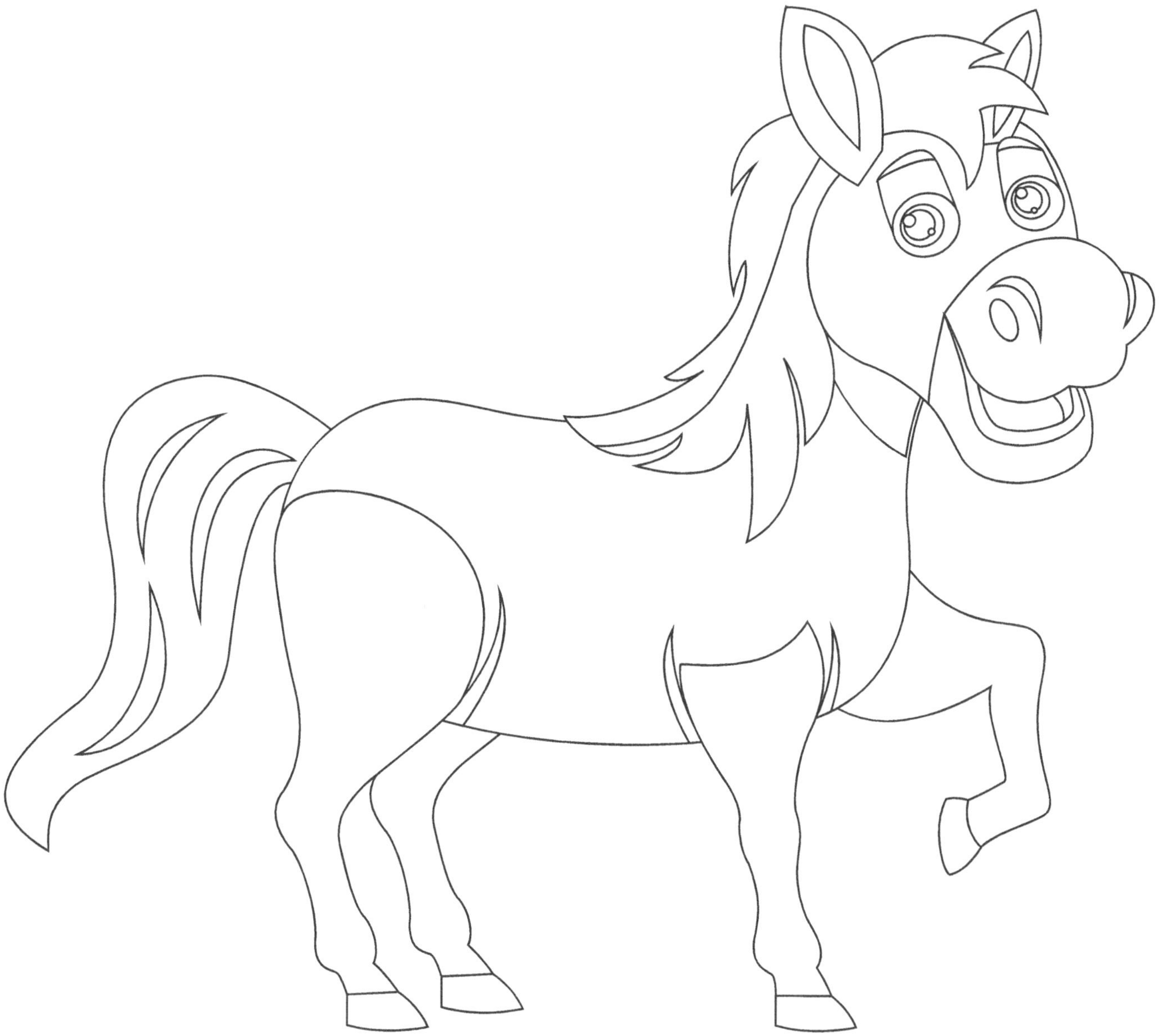

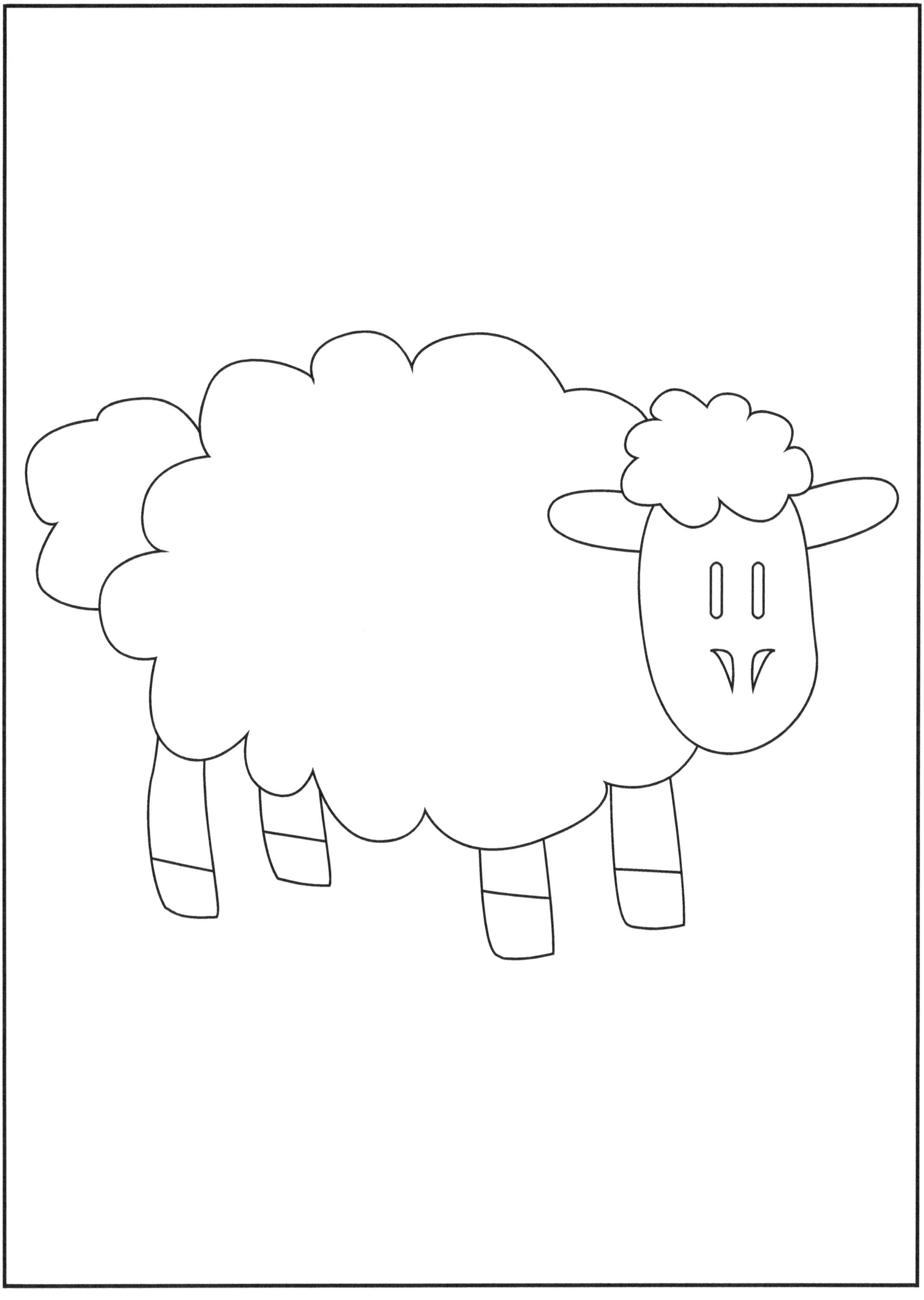

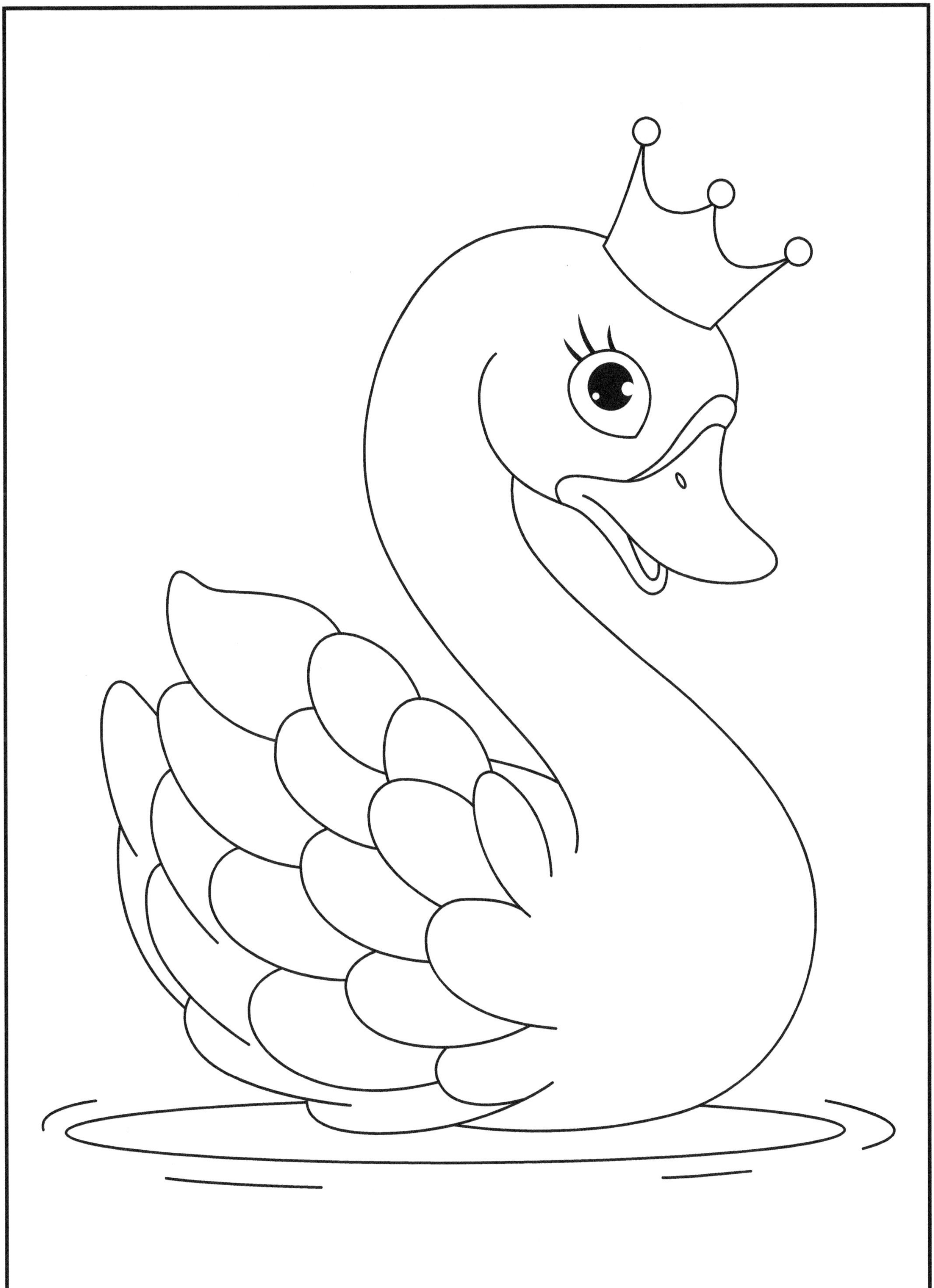

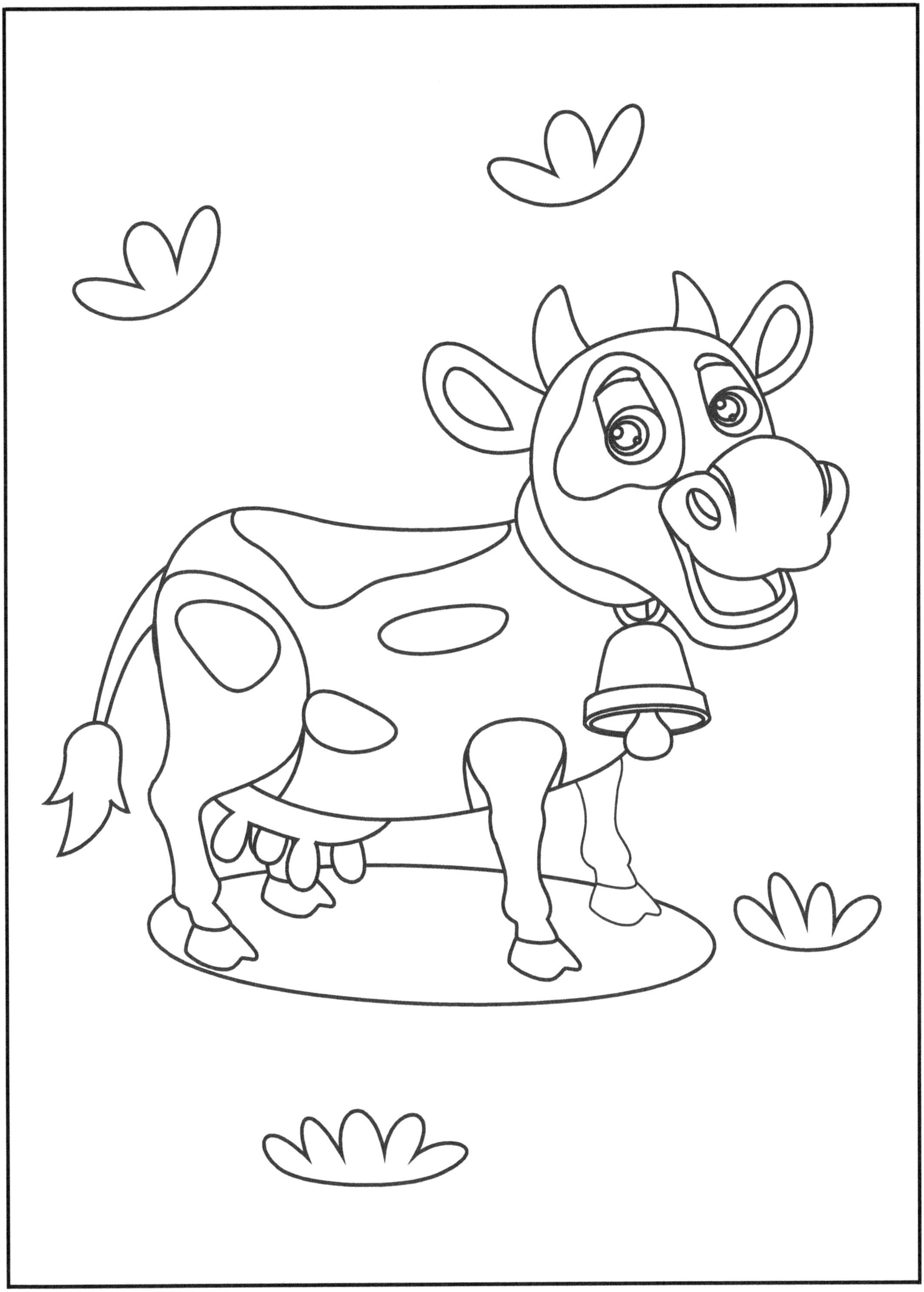

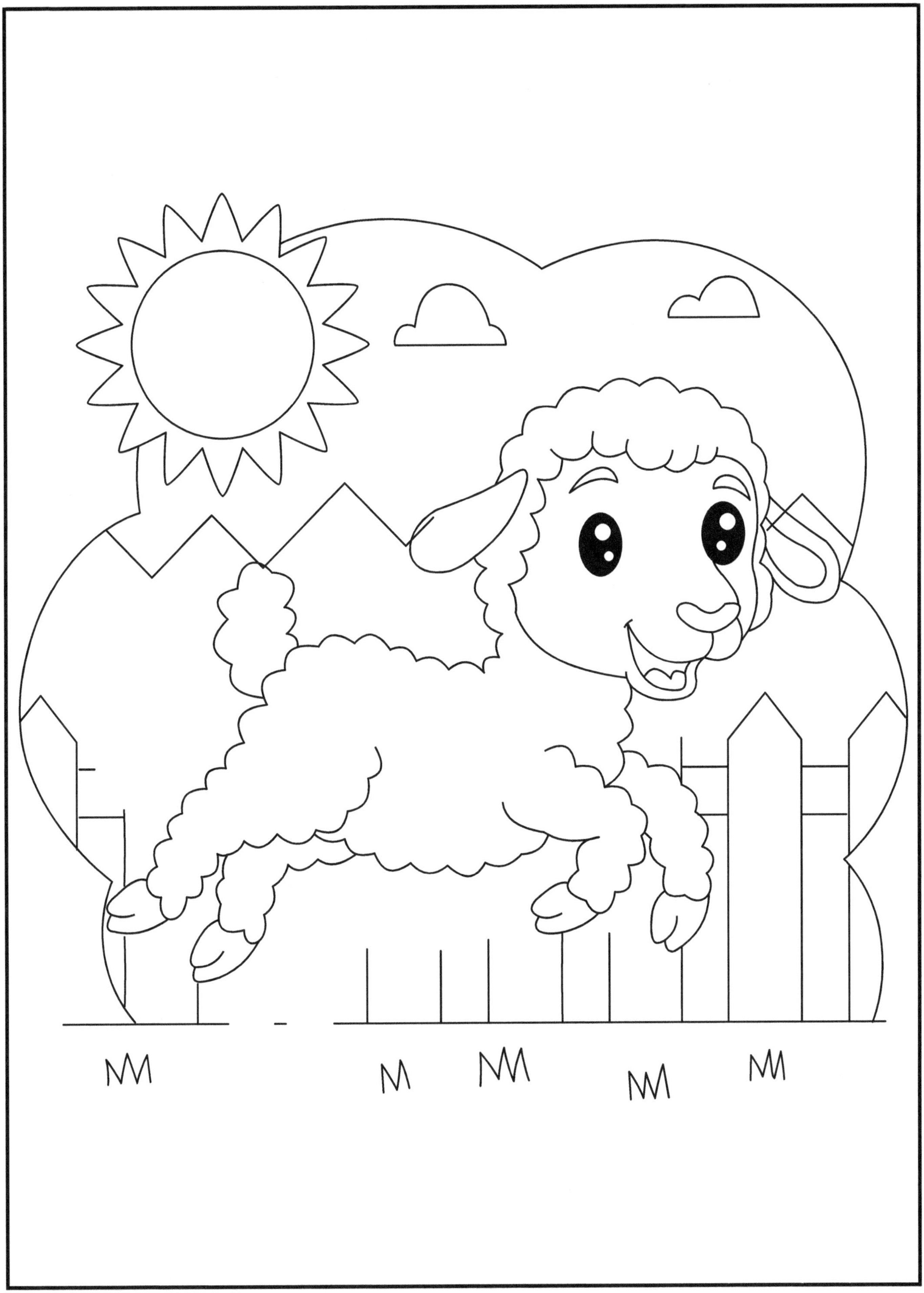

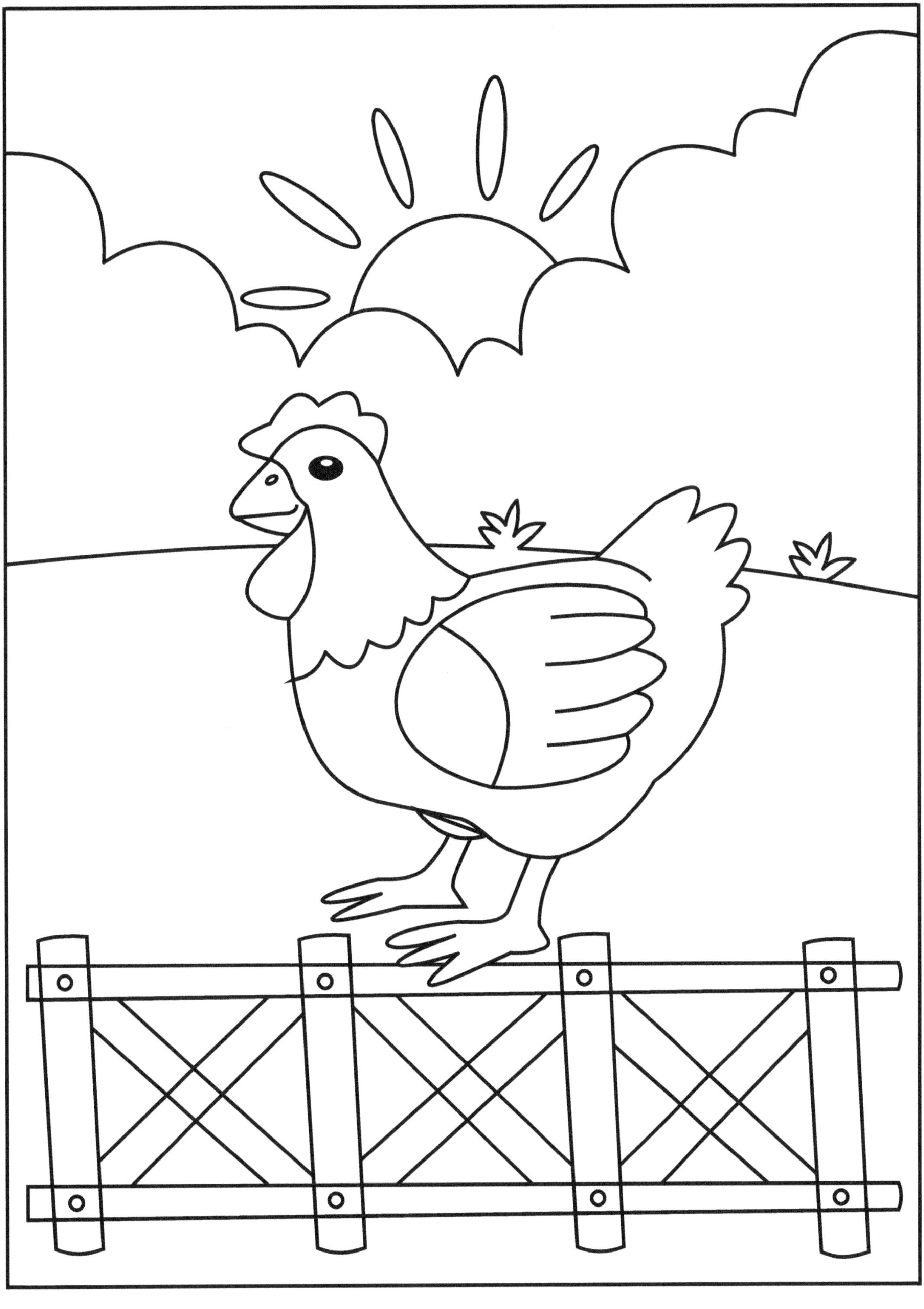

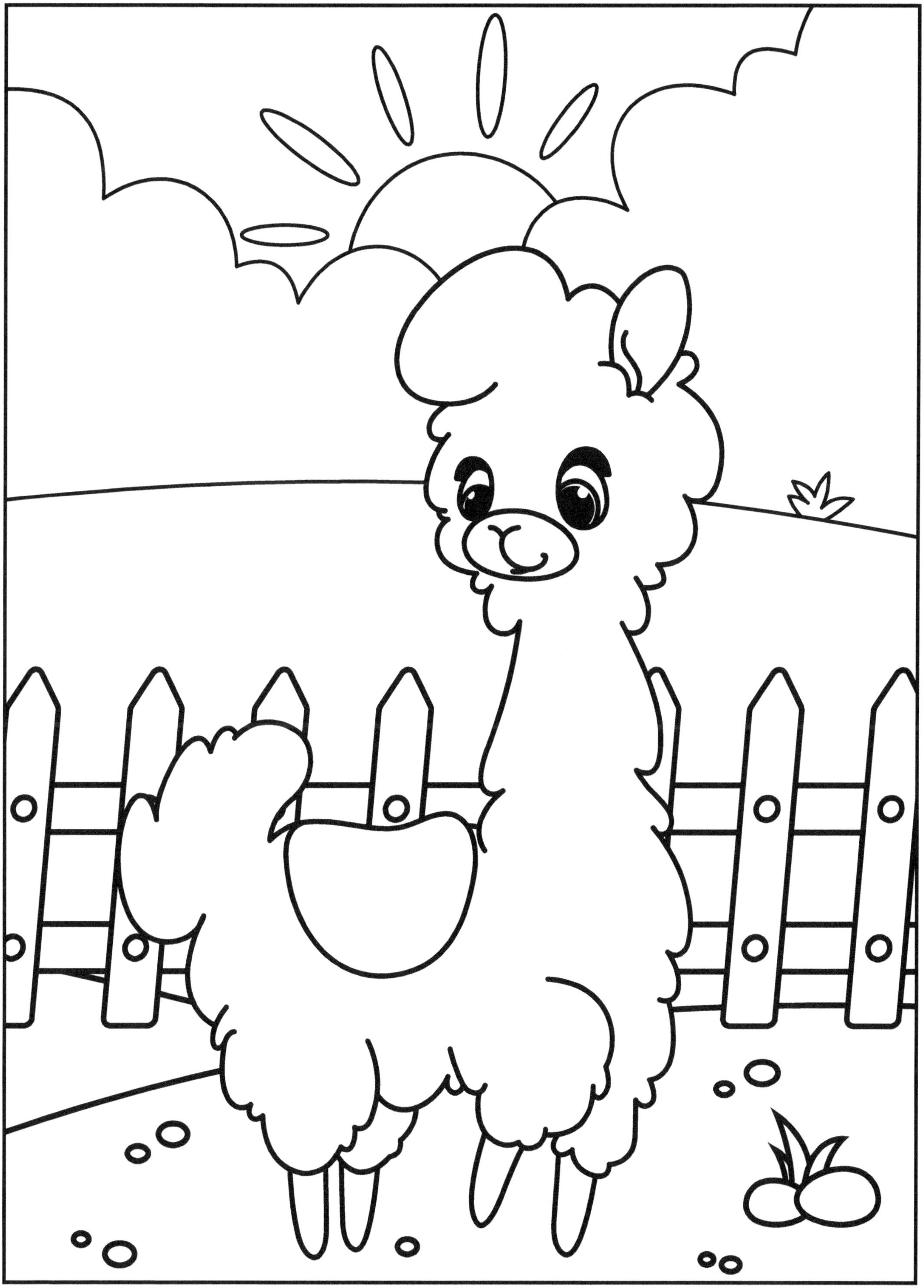

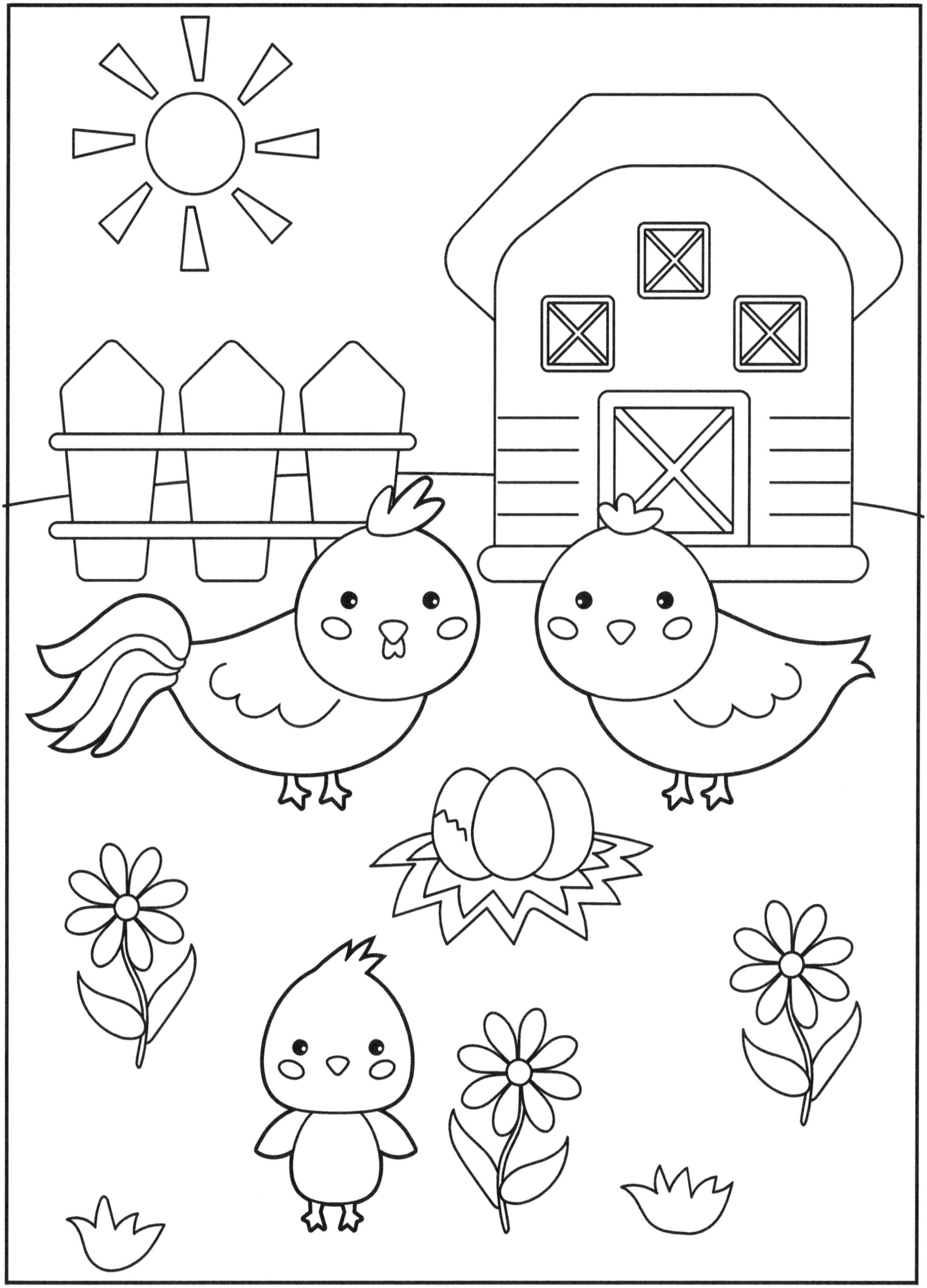

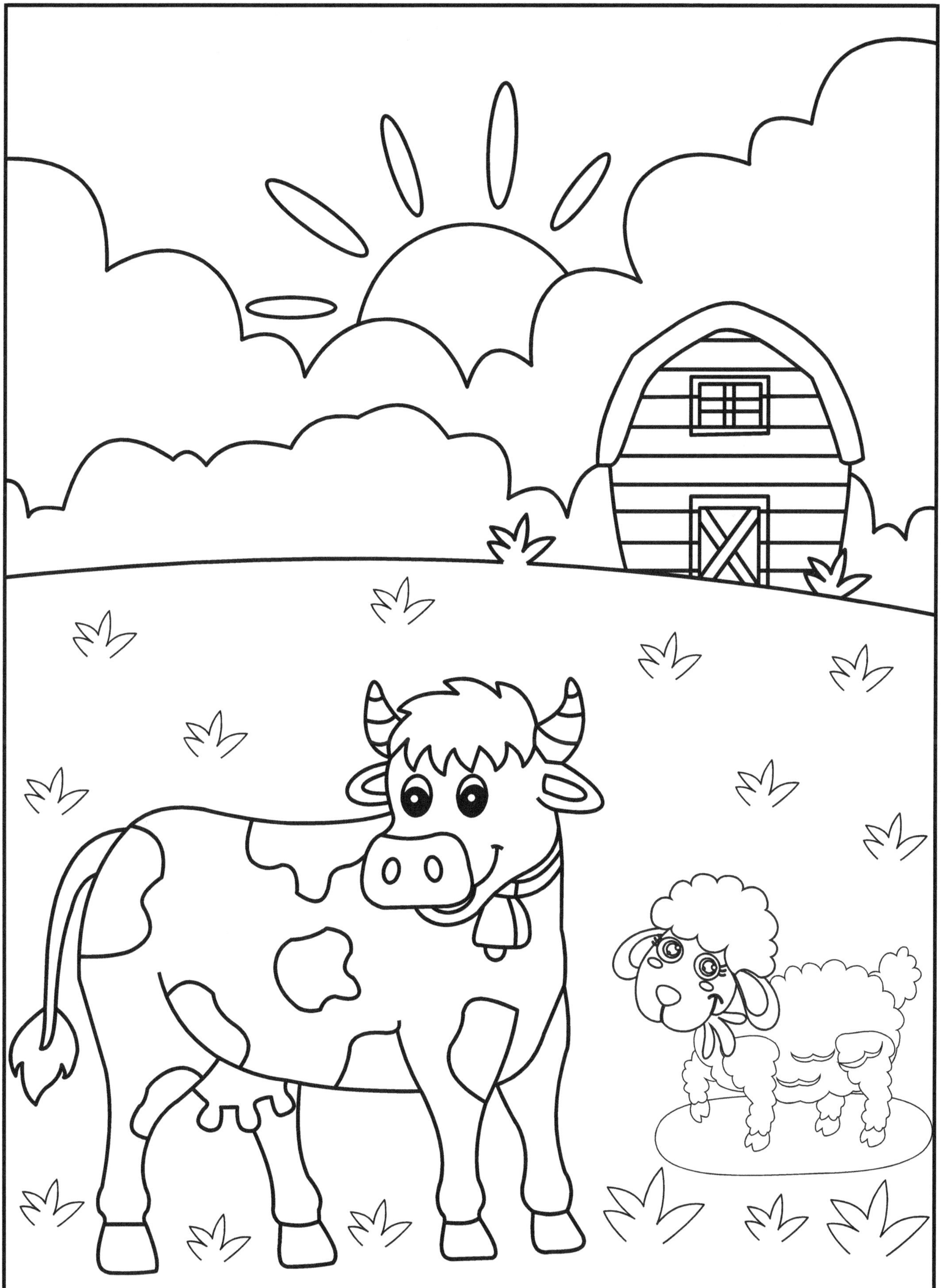

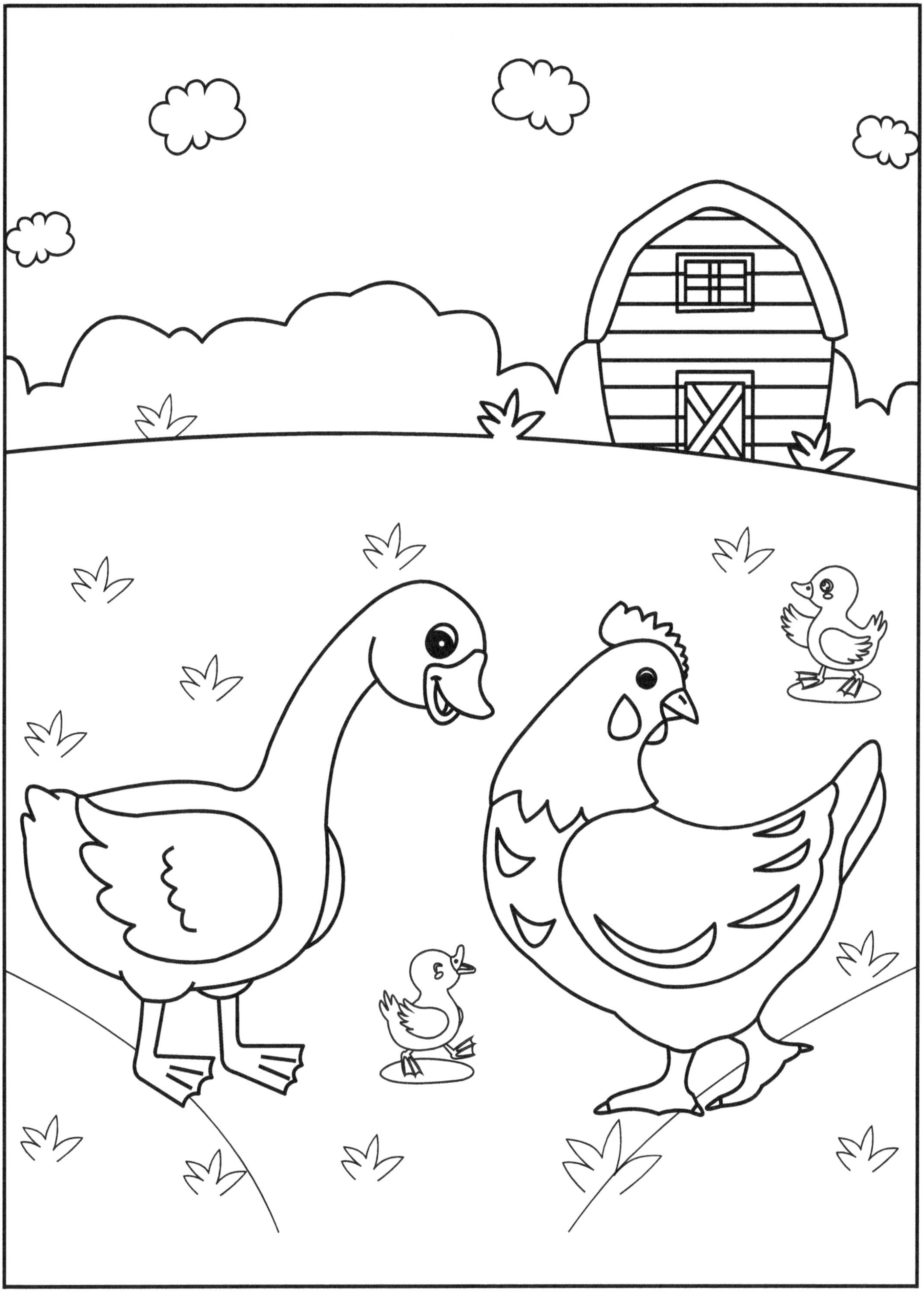

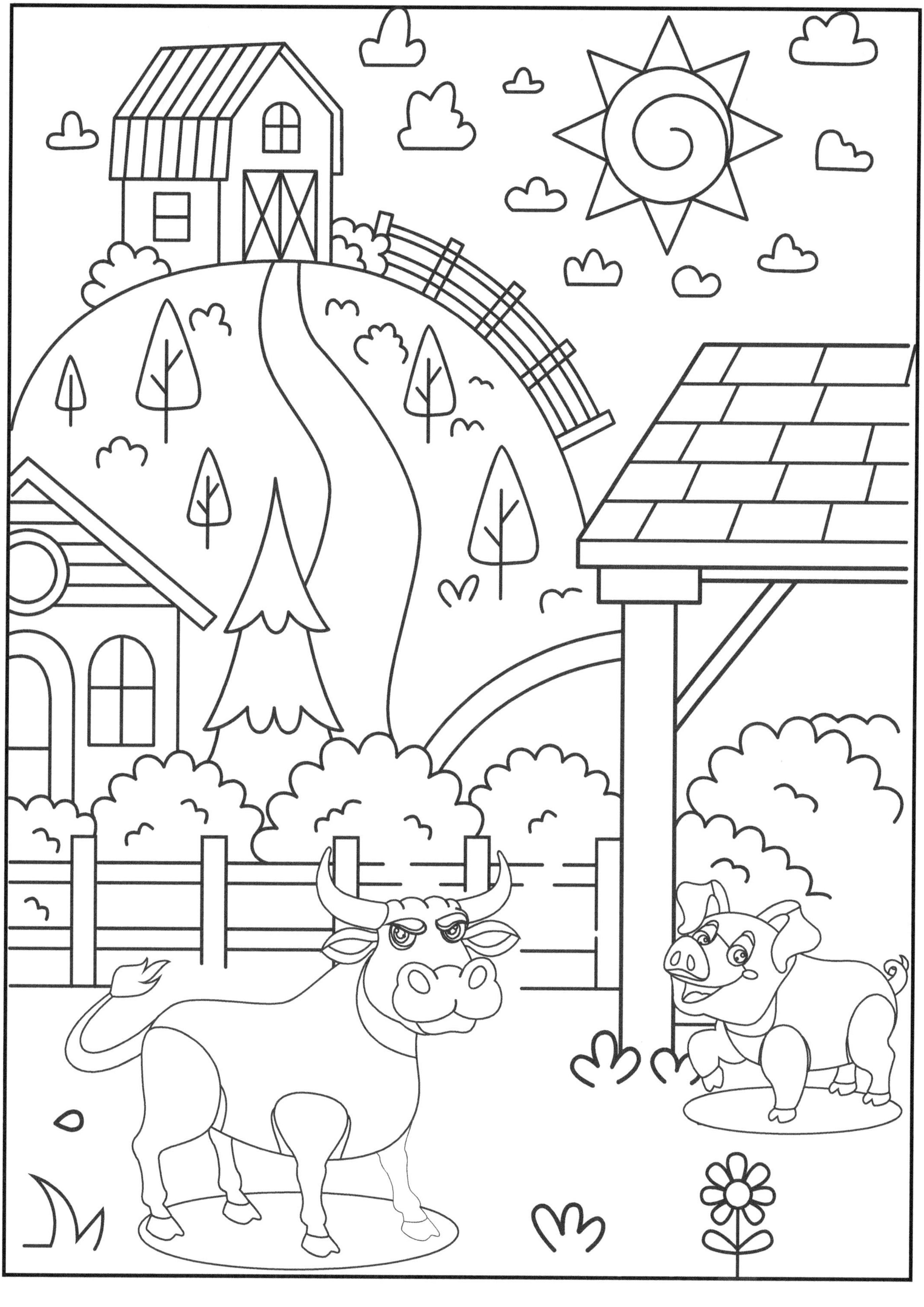

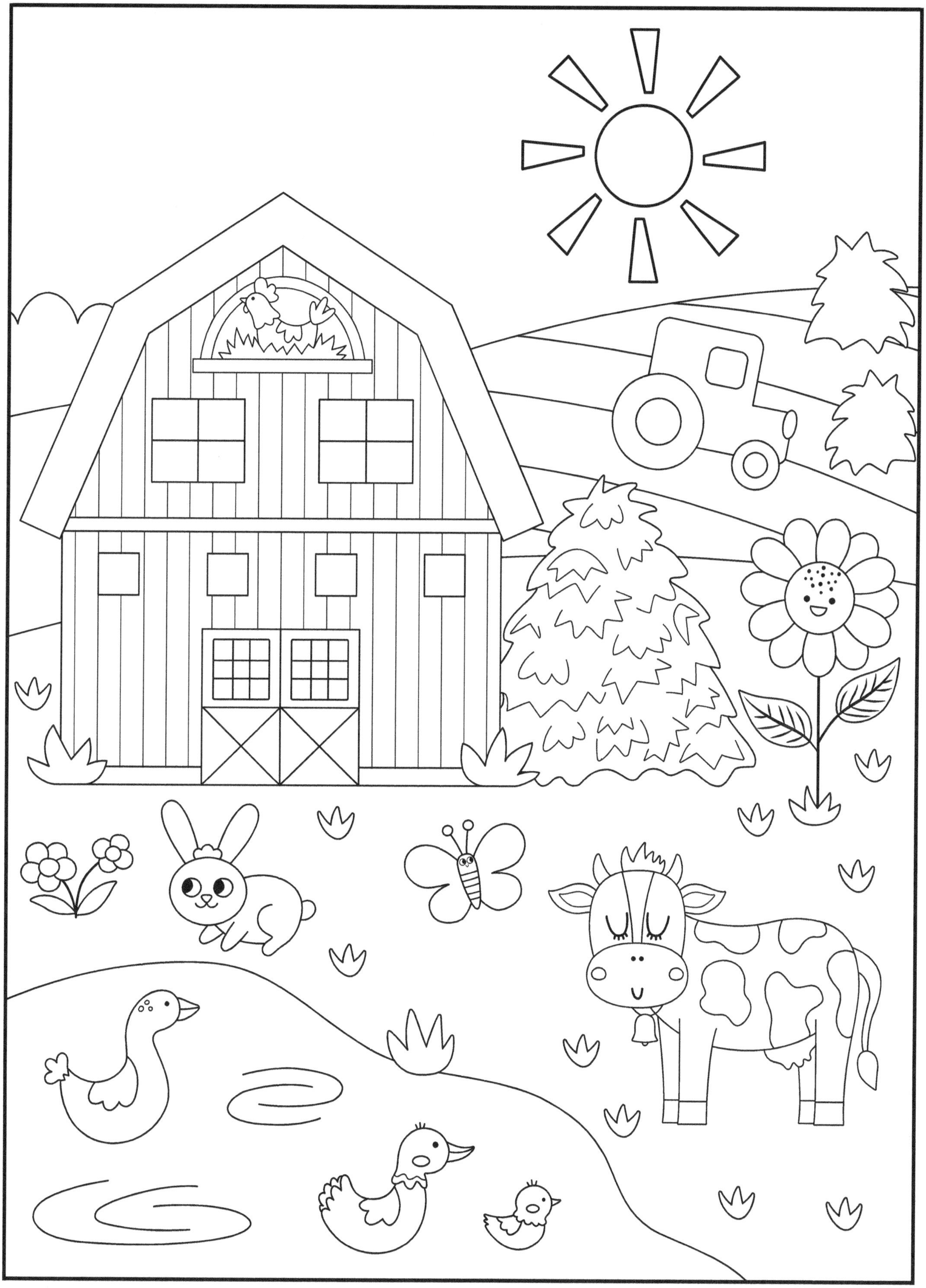

Sea Animals

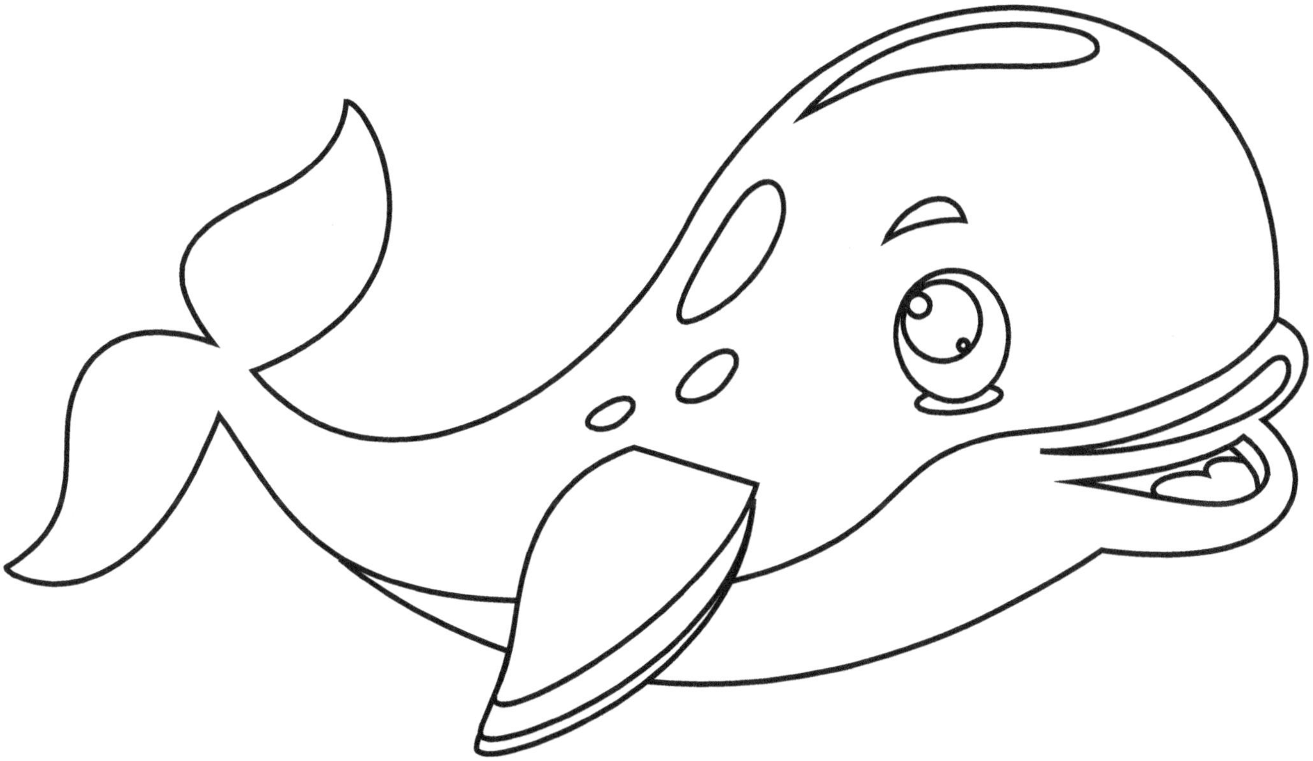

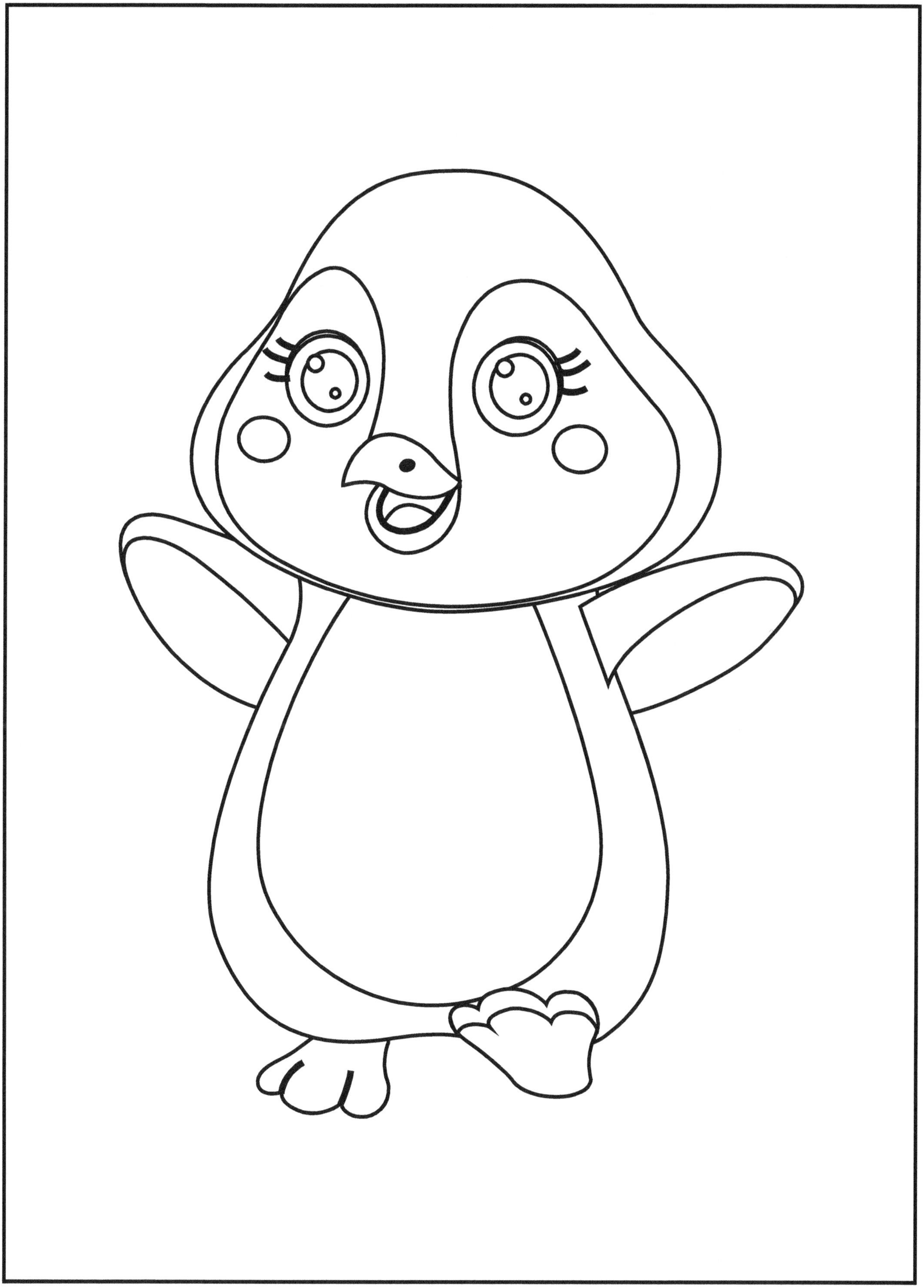

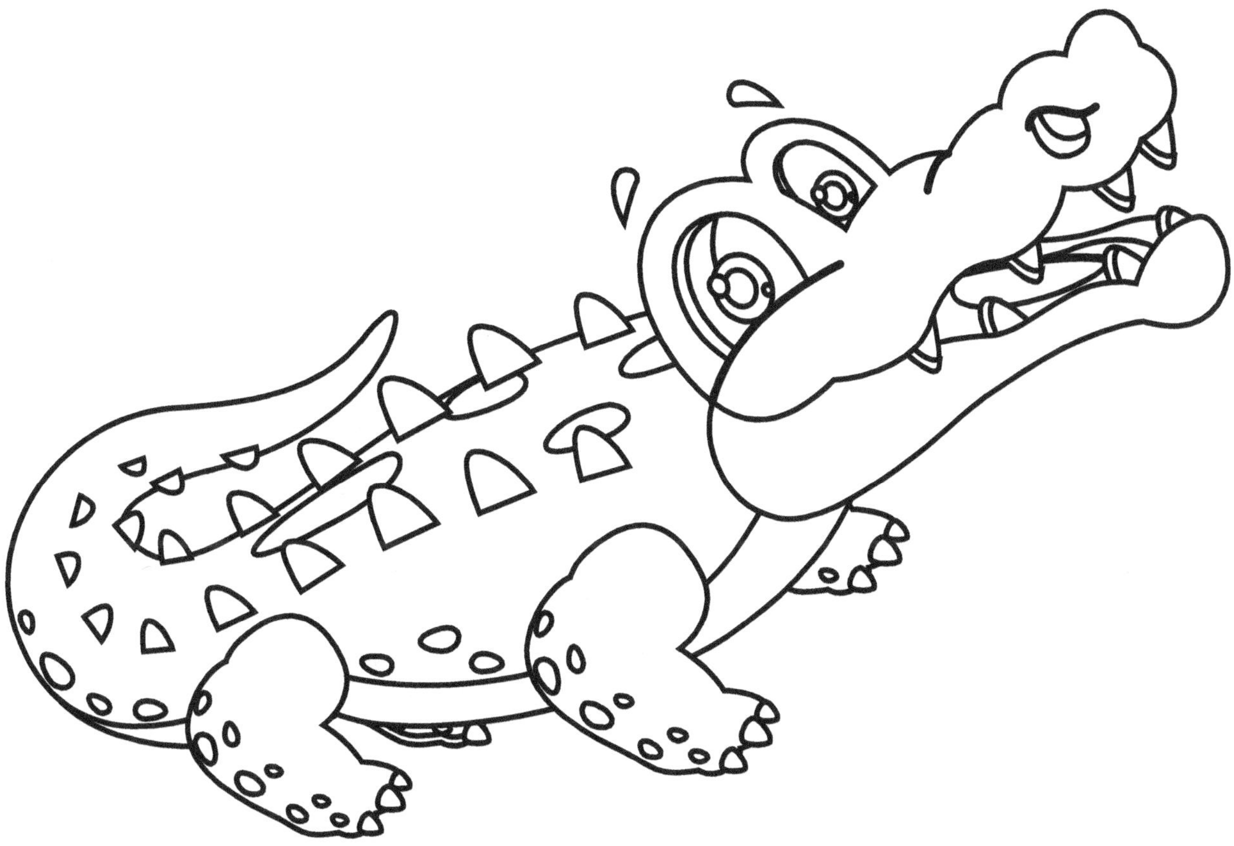

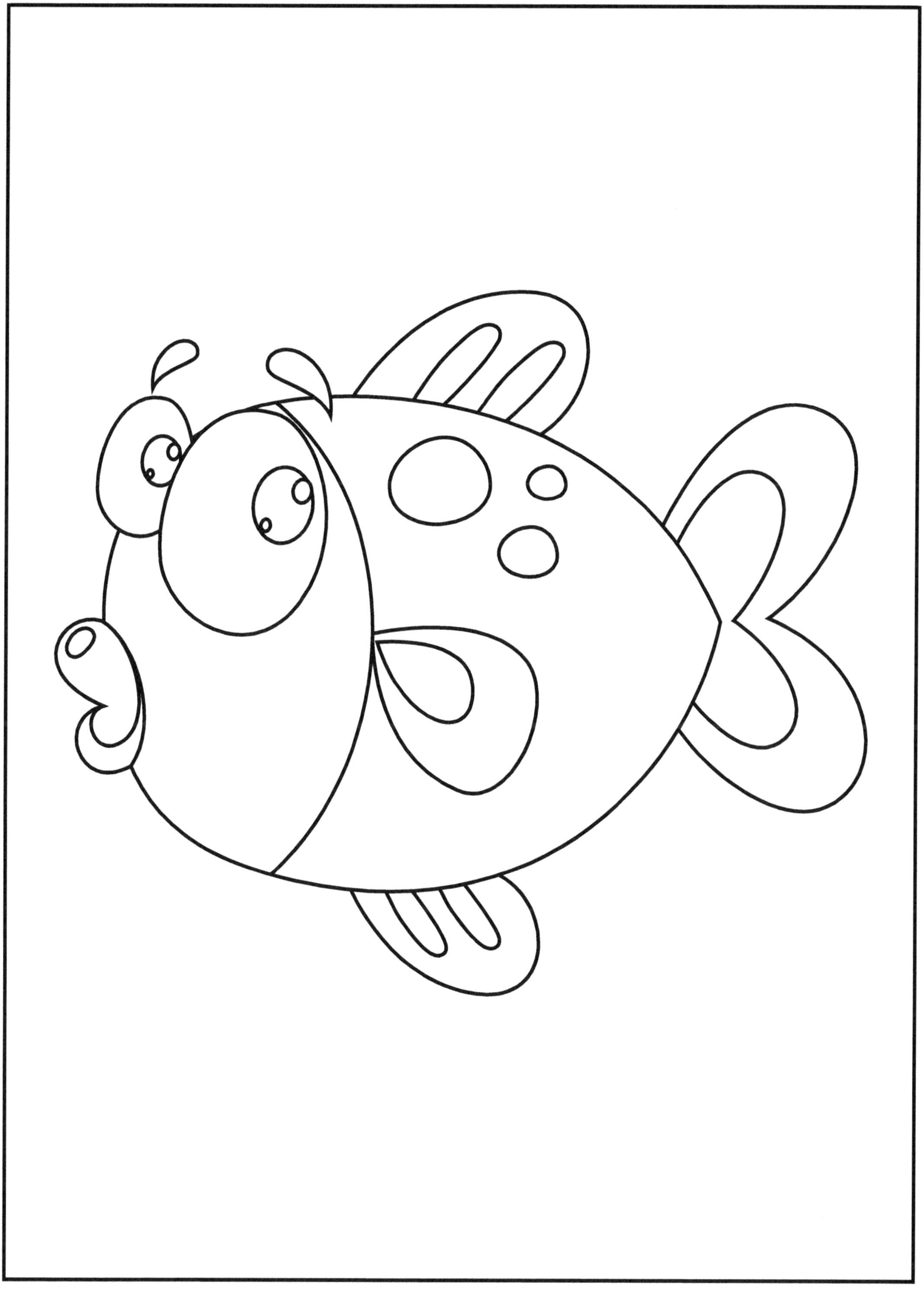

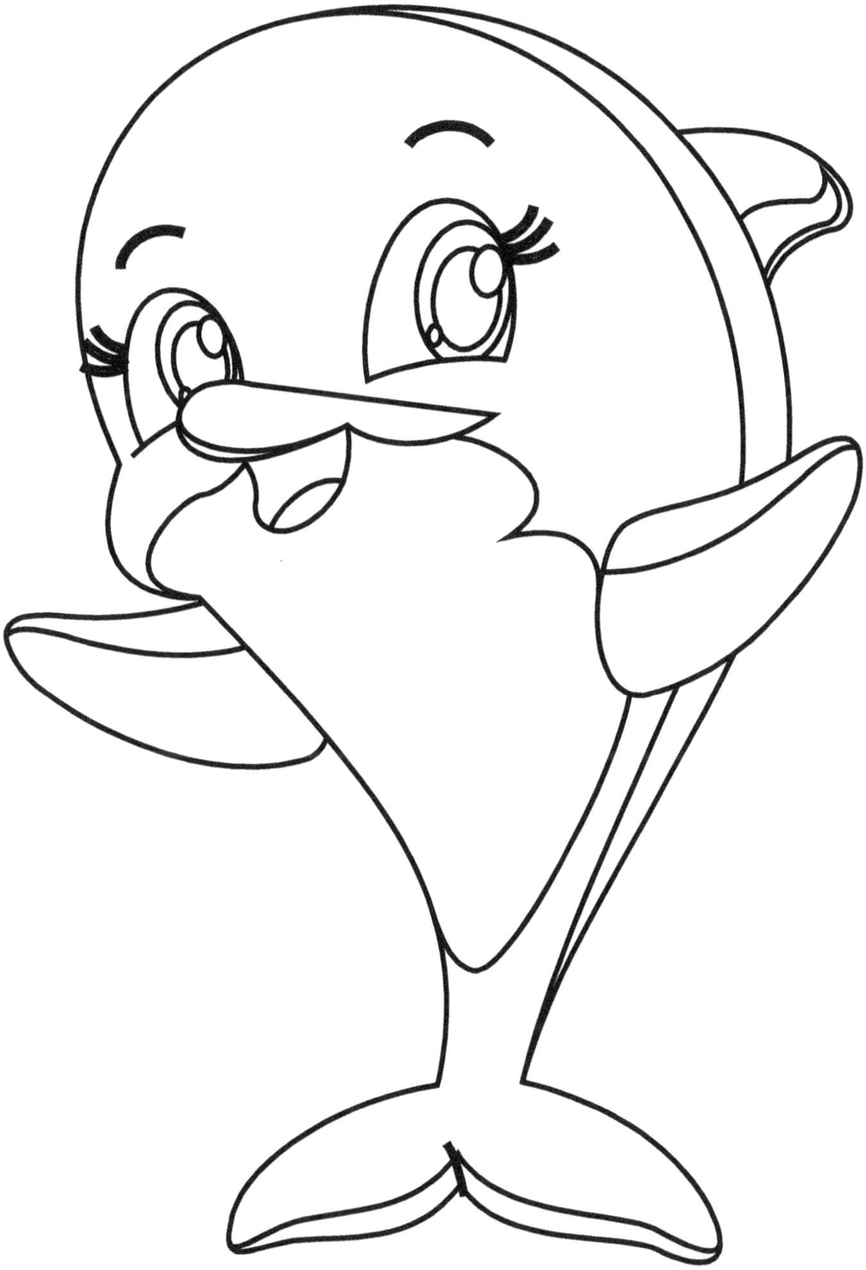

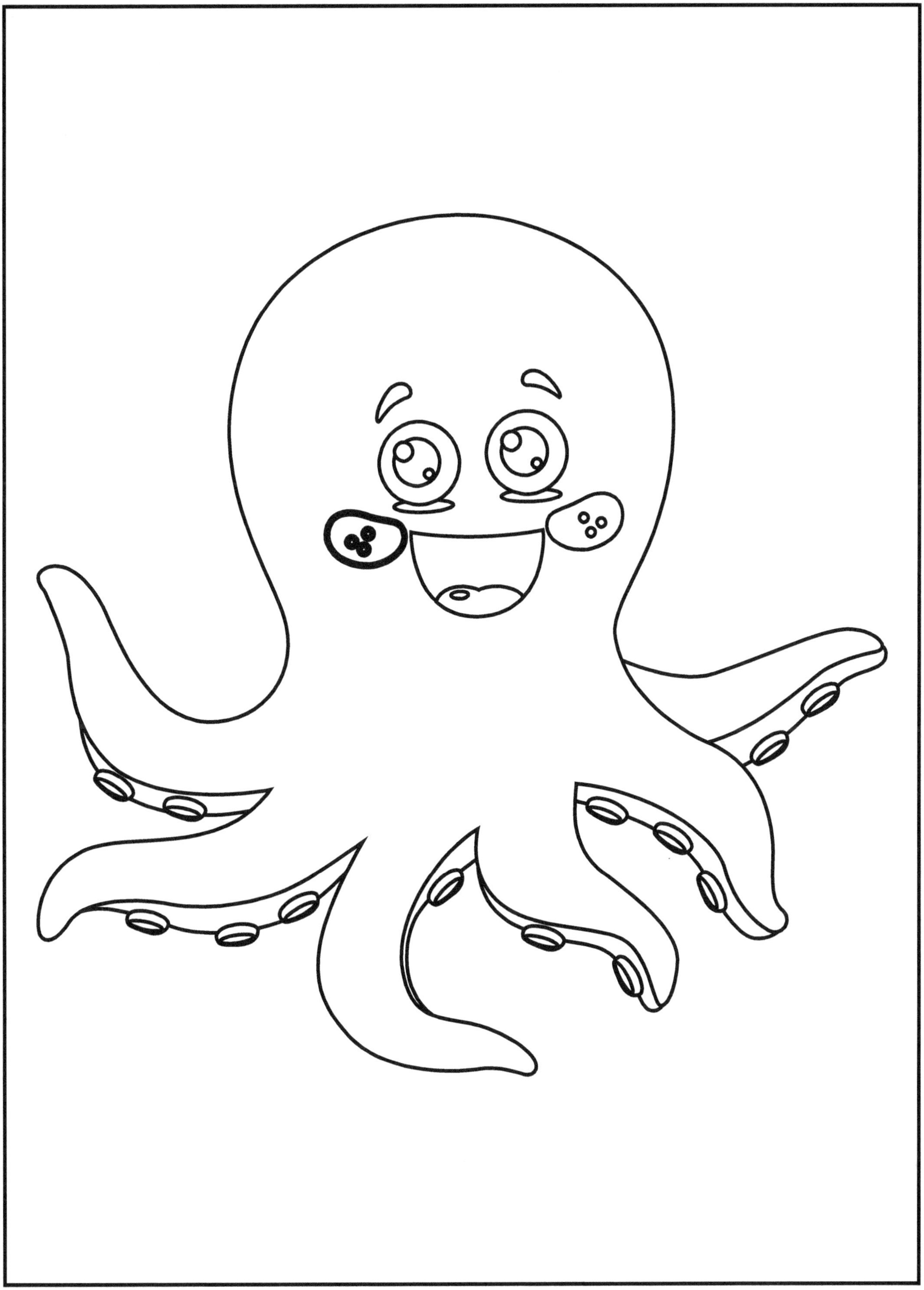

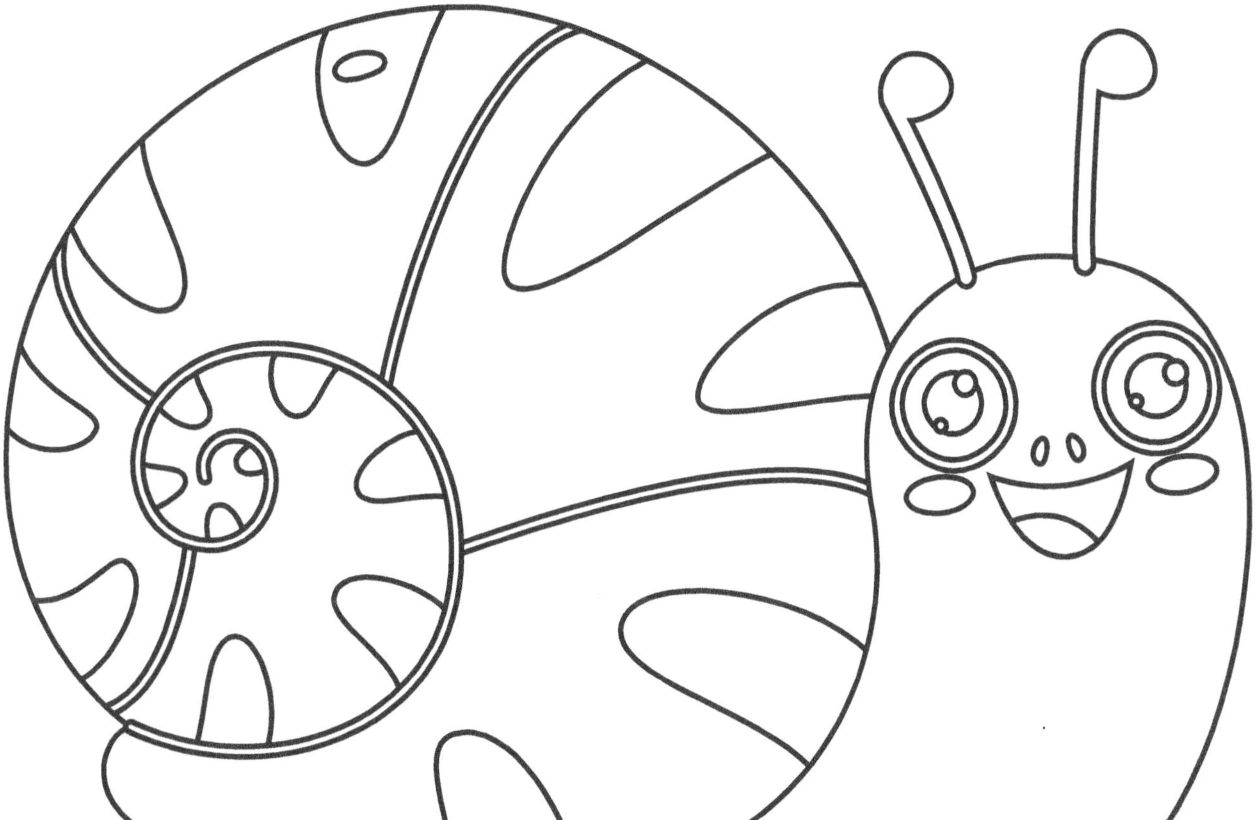

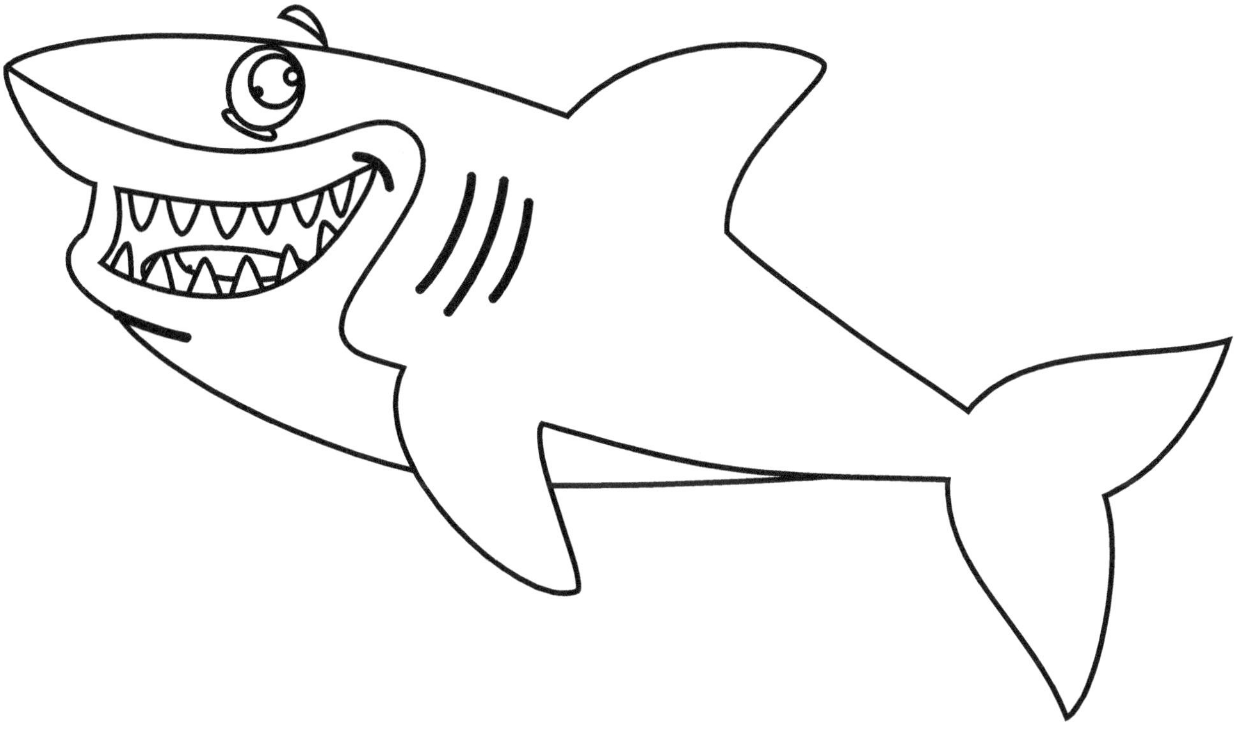

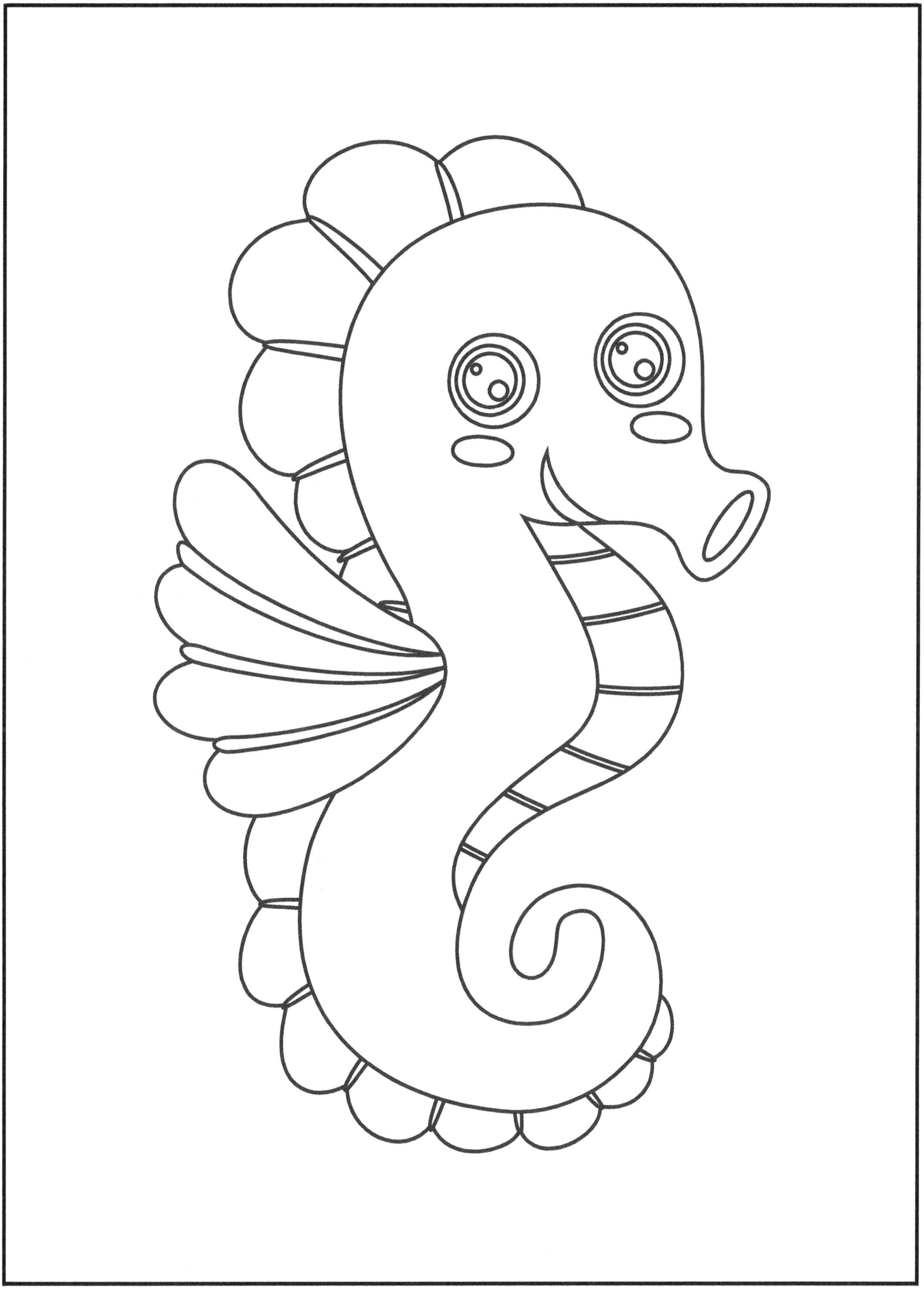

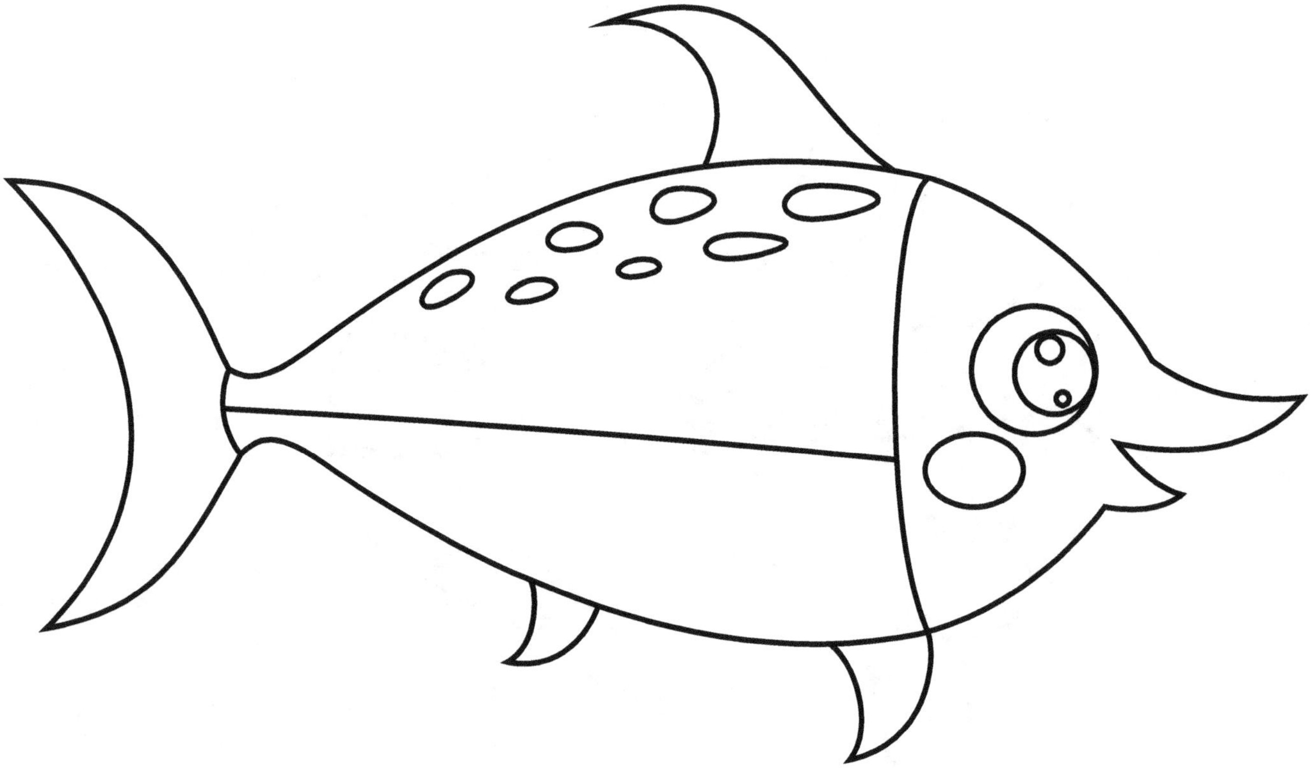

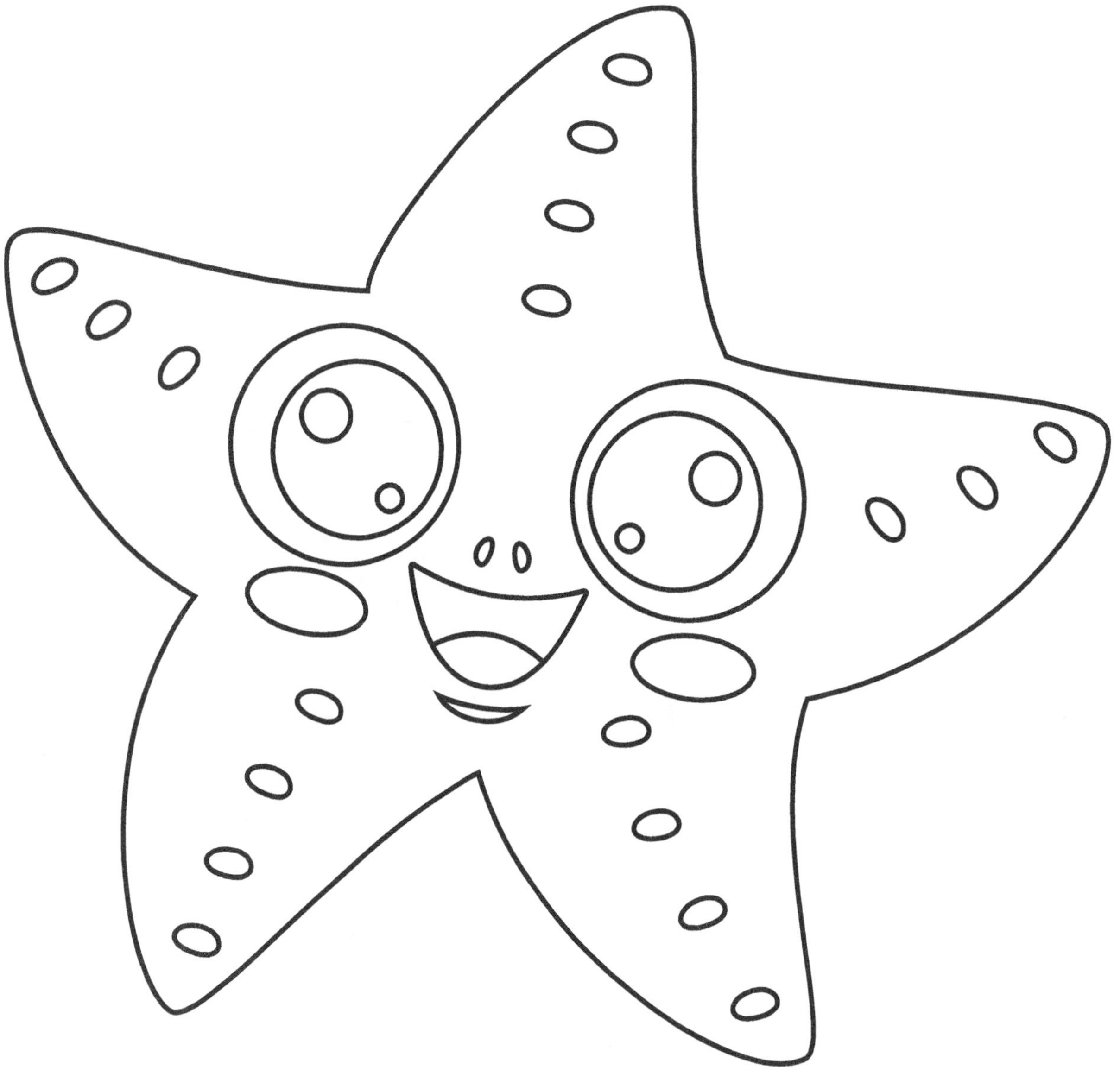

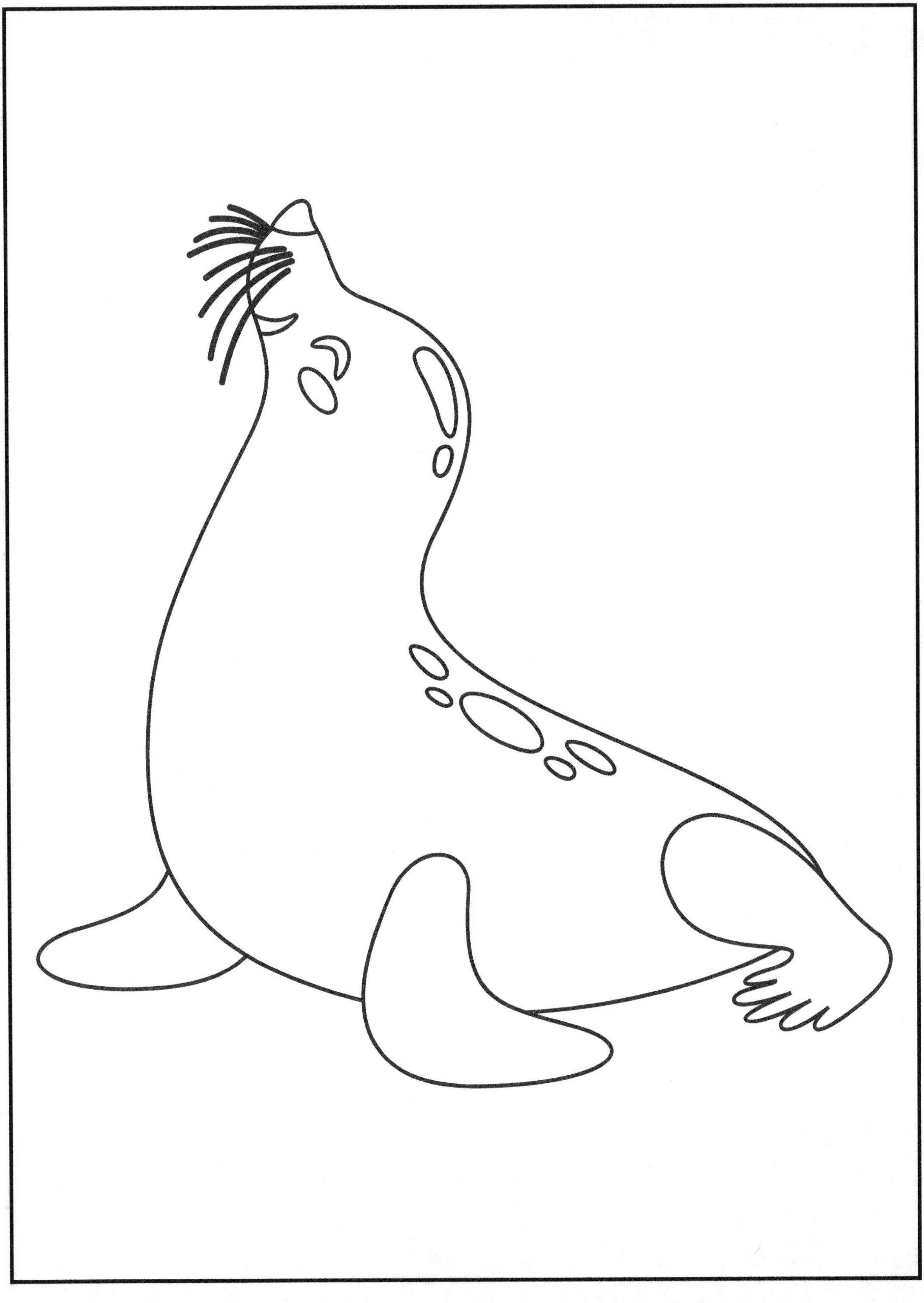

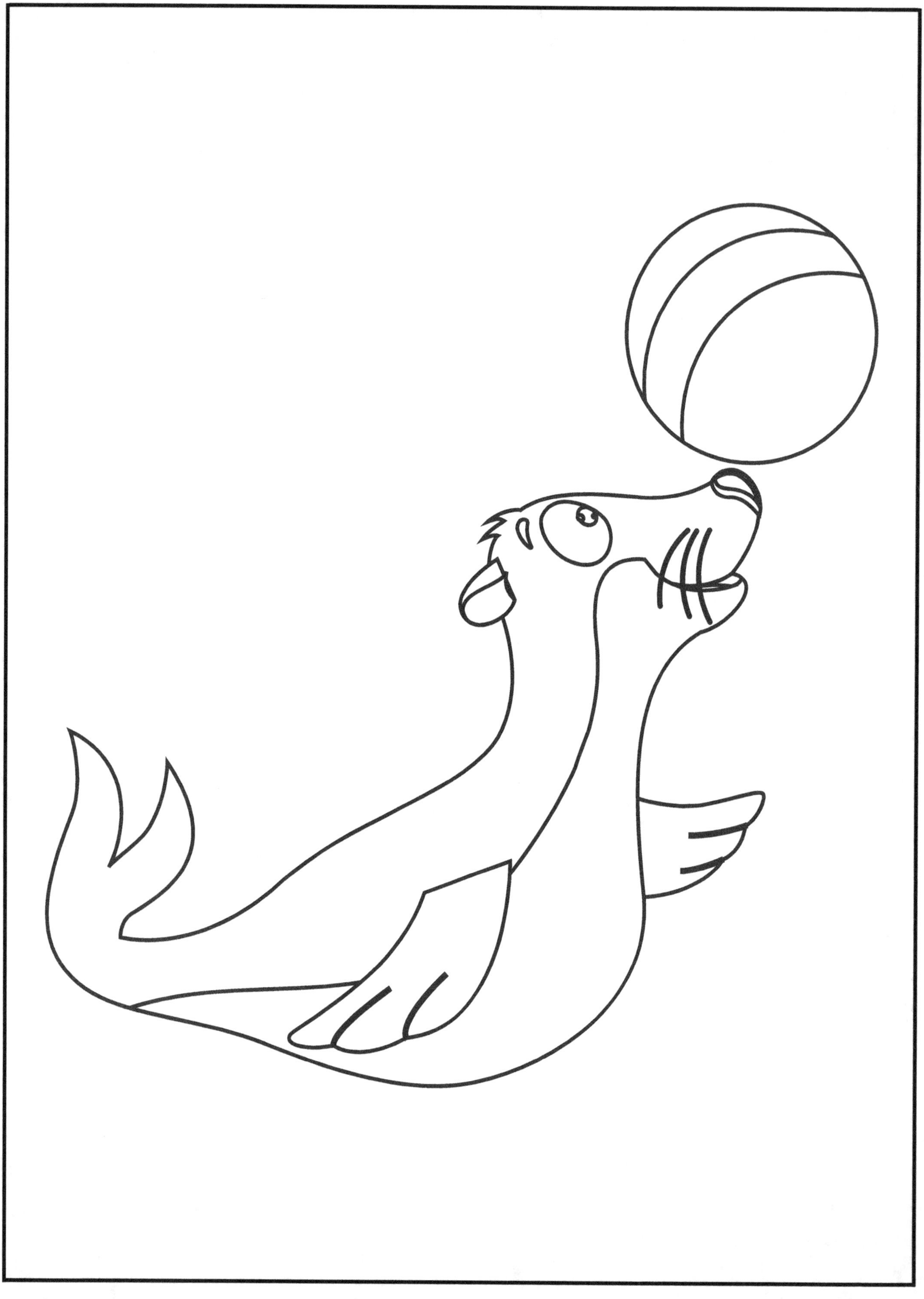

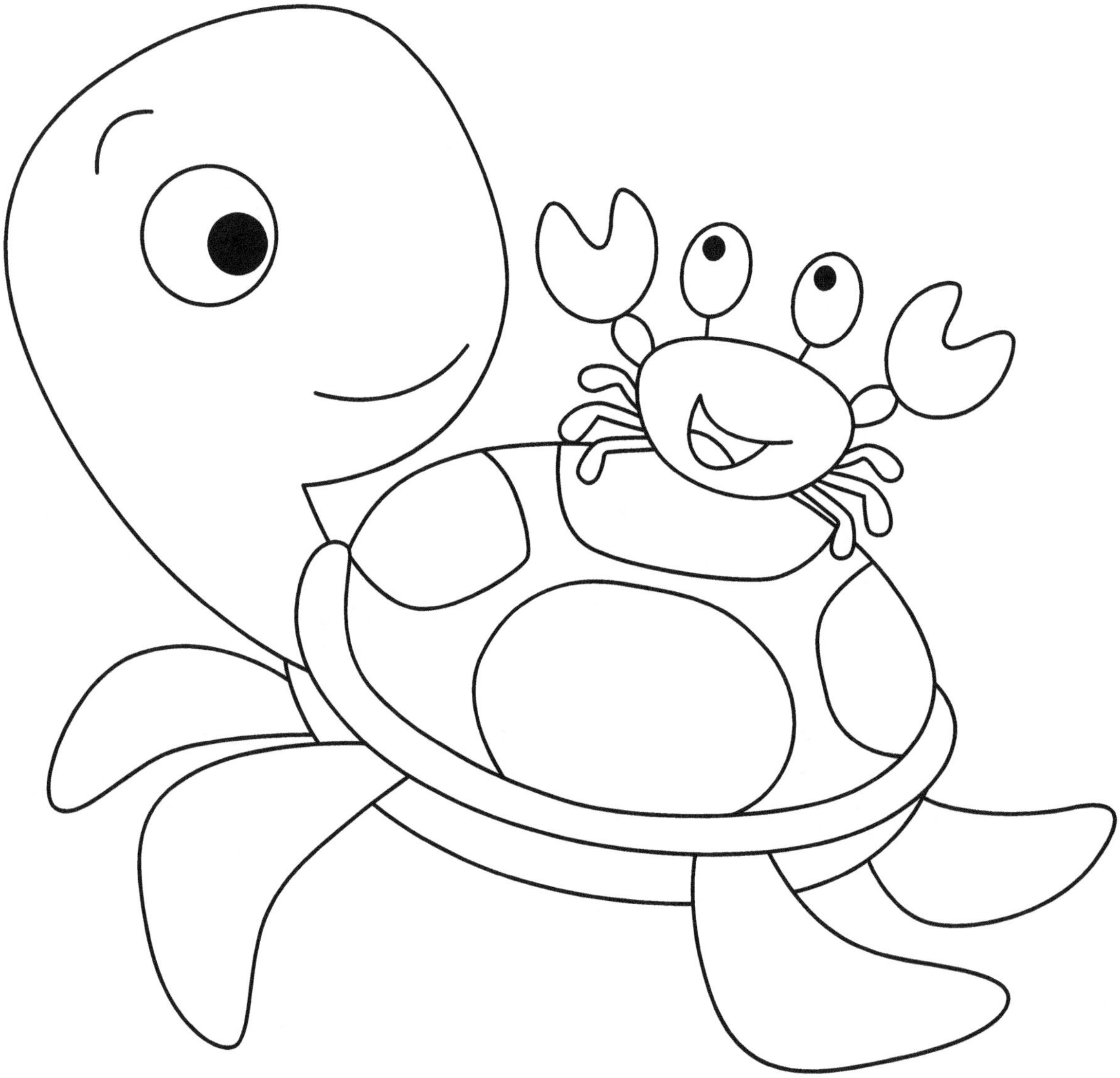

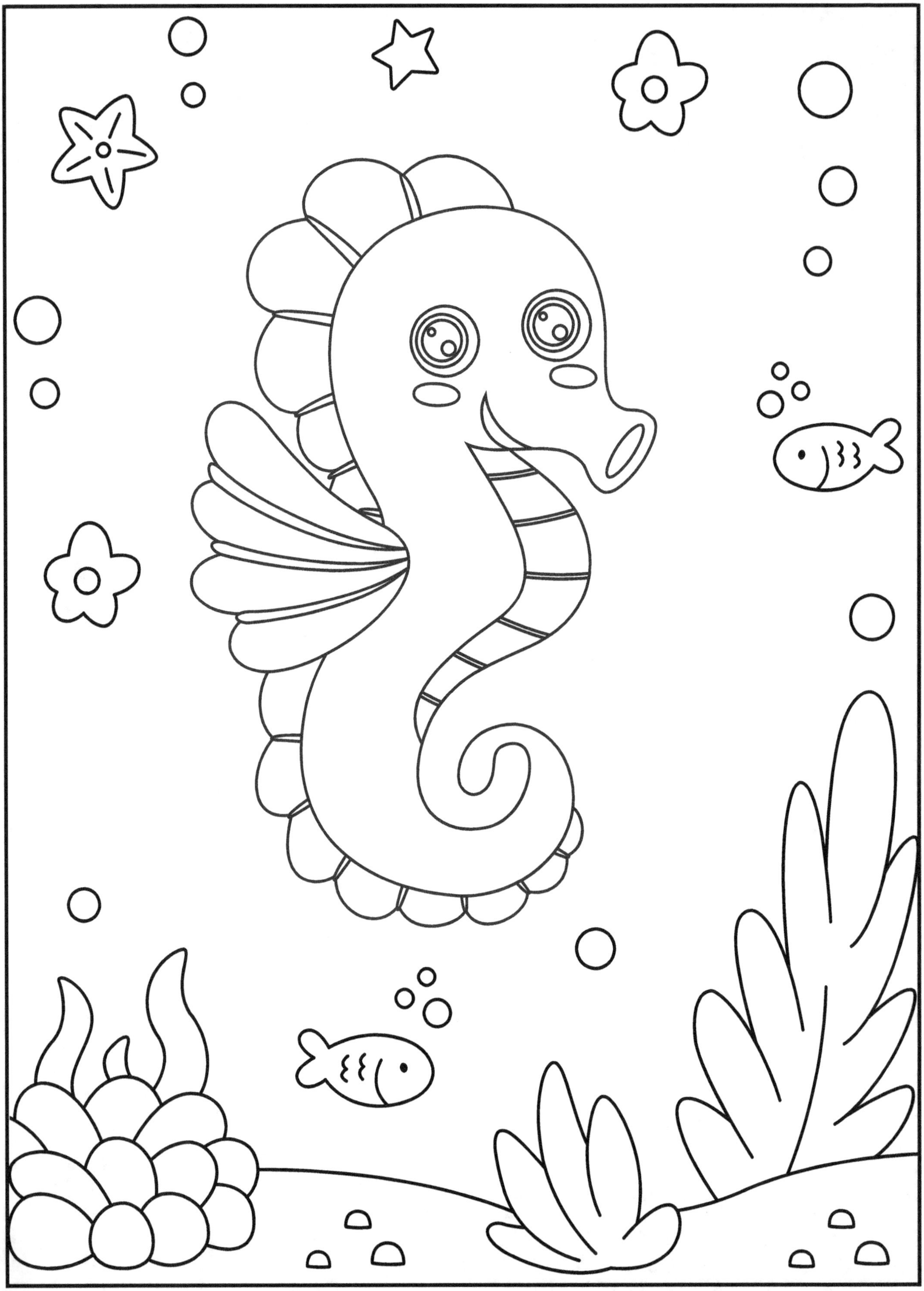

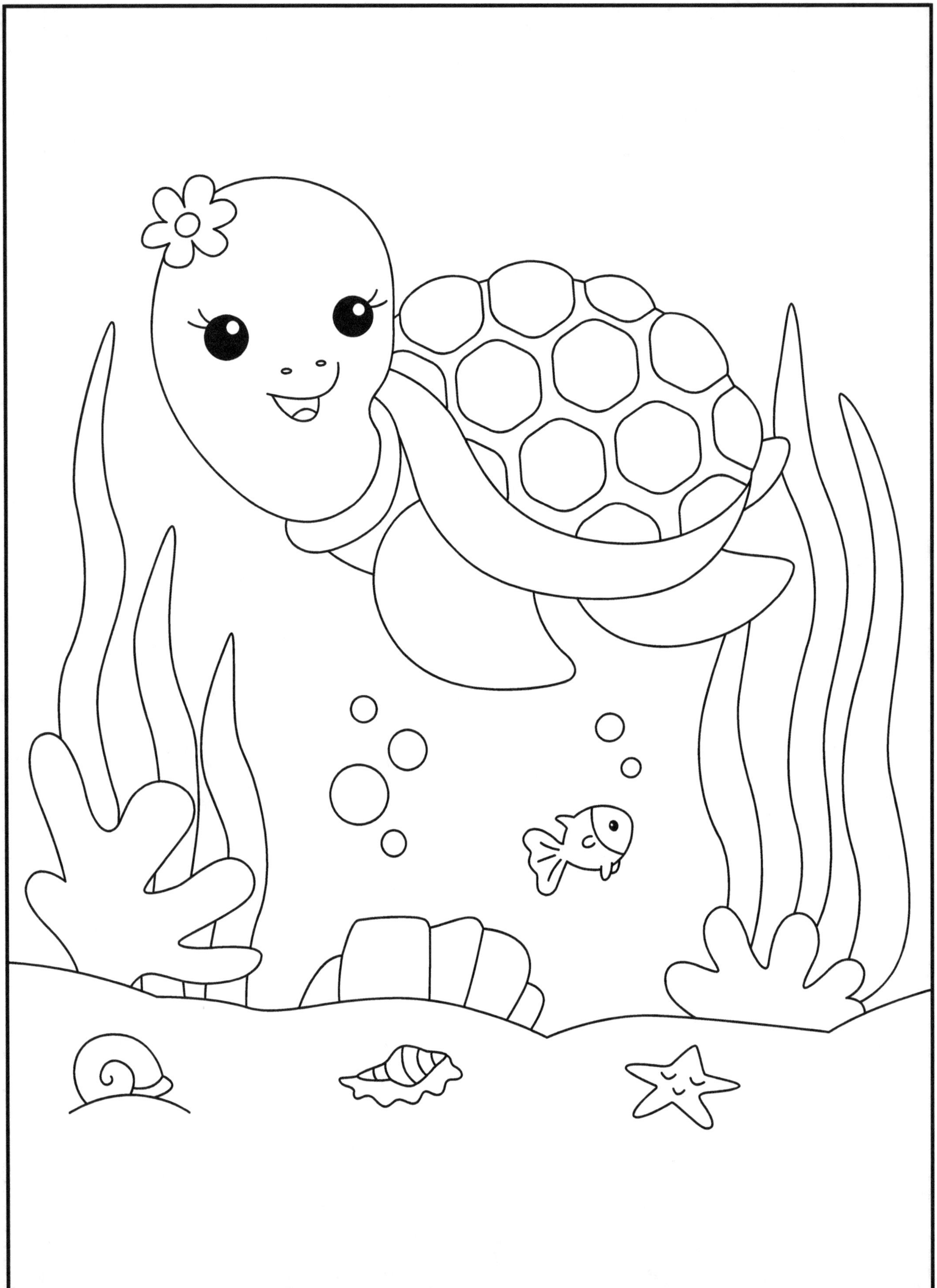

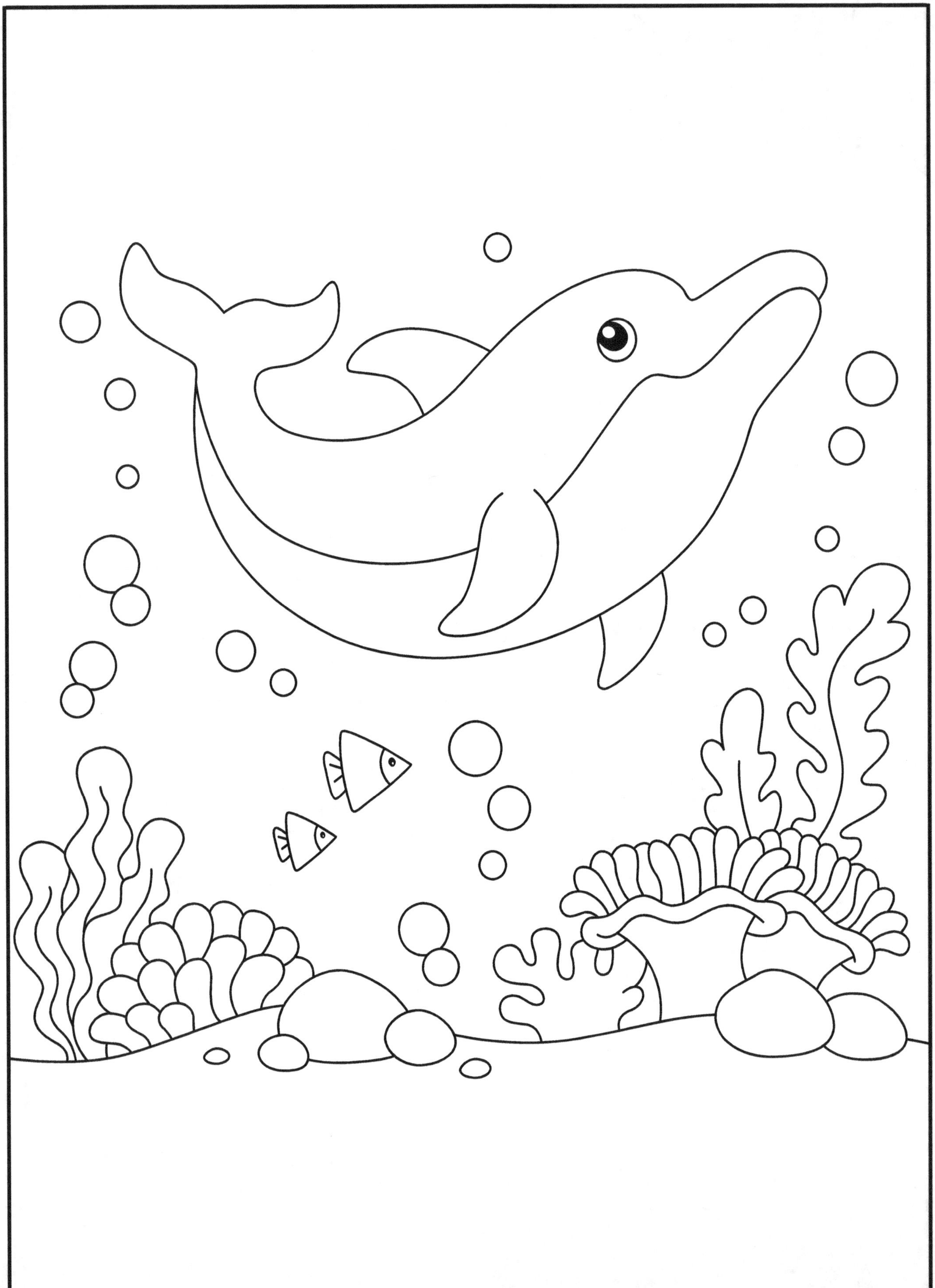

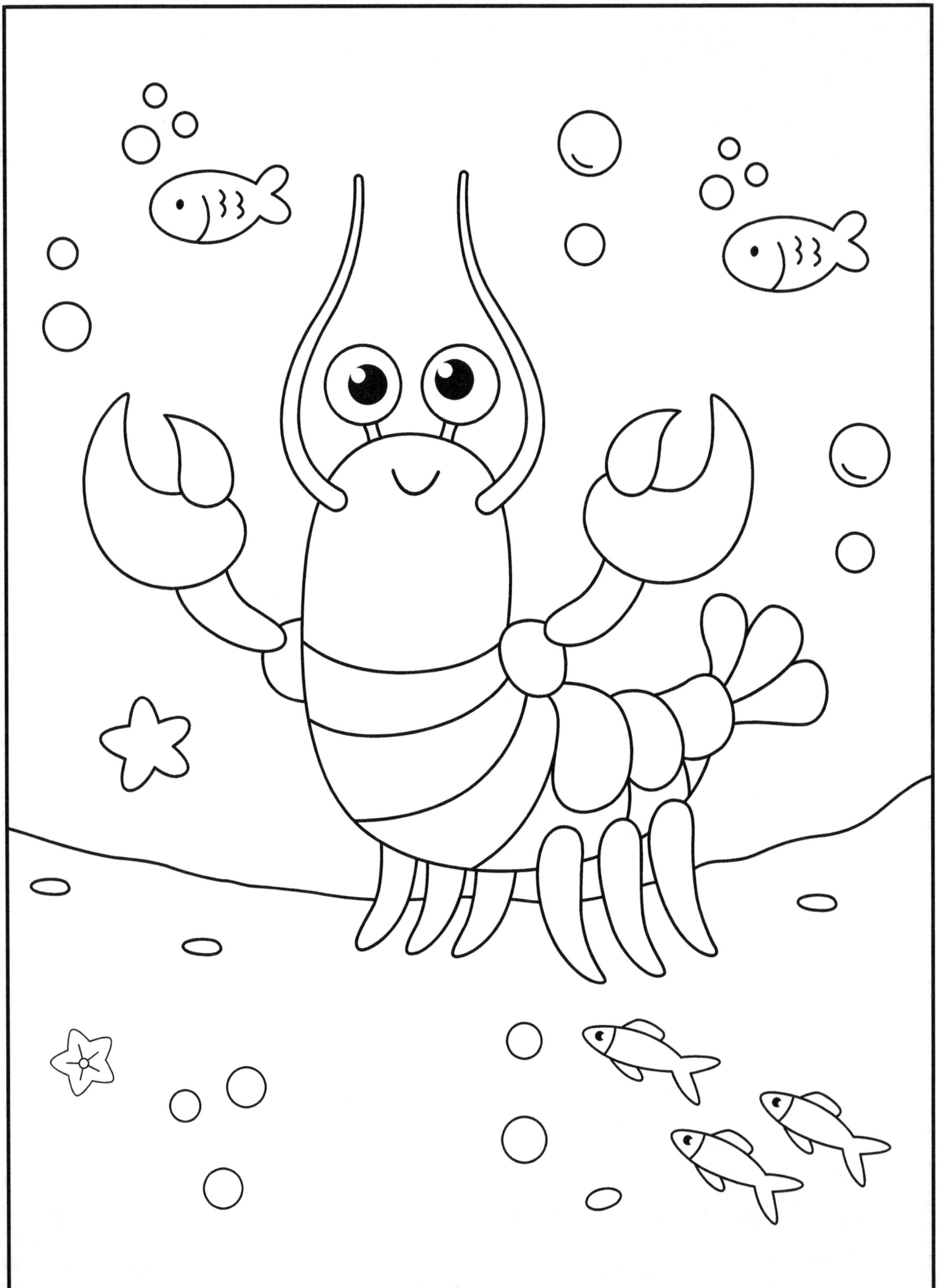

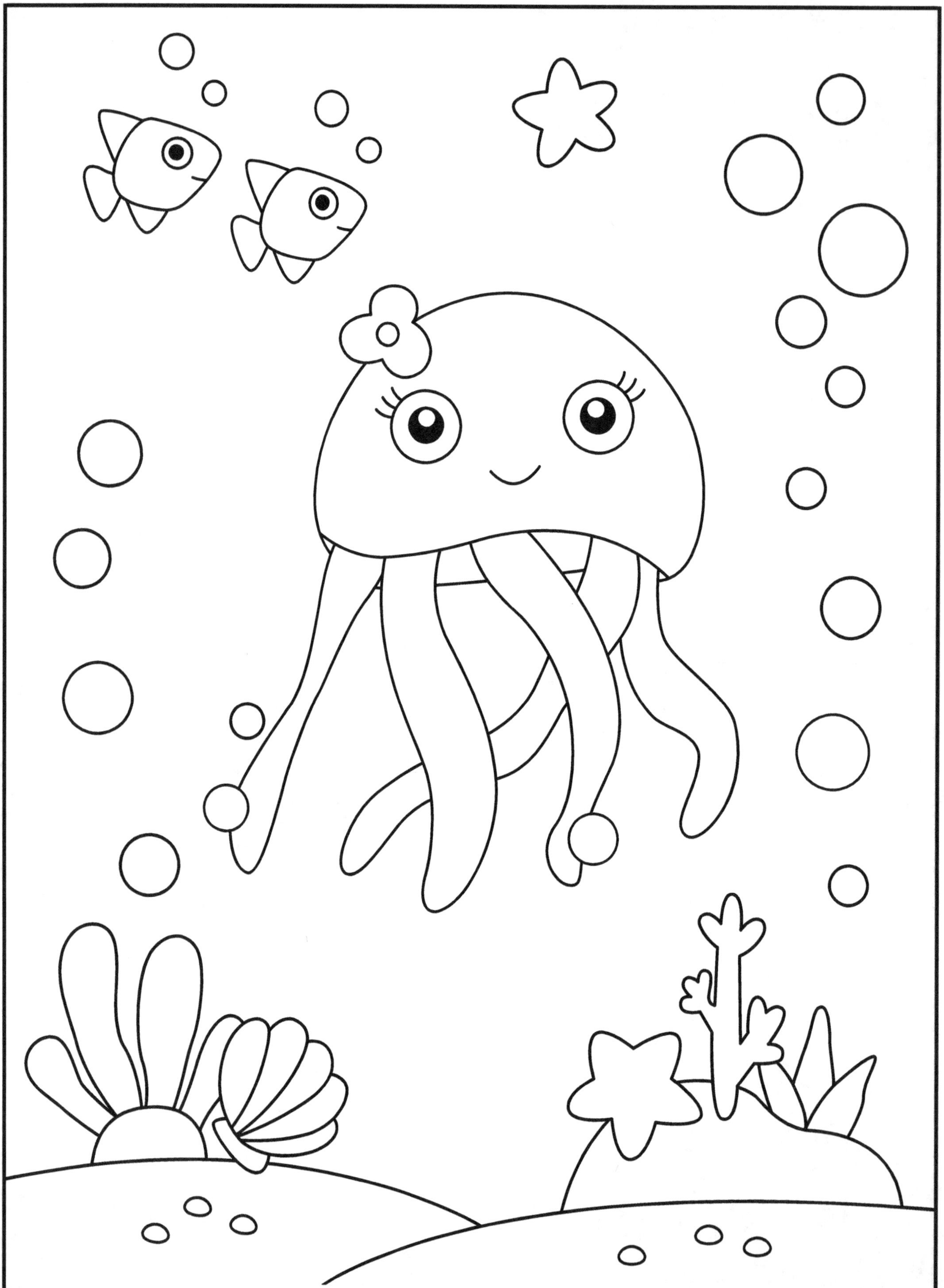

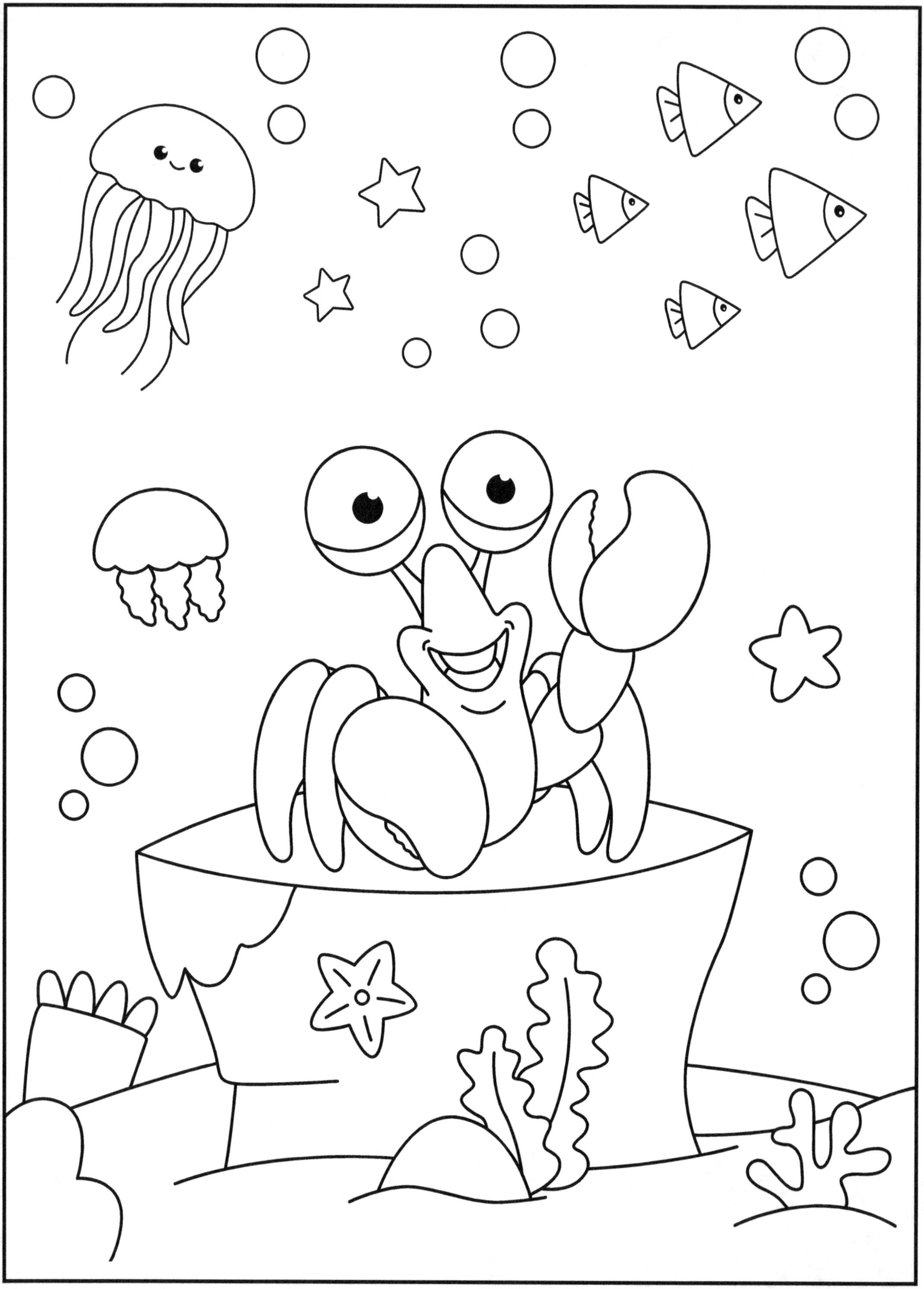

Bug
&
Insects

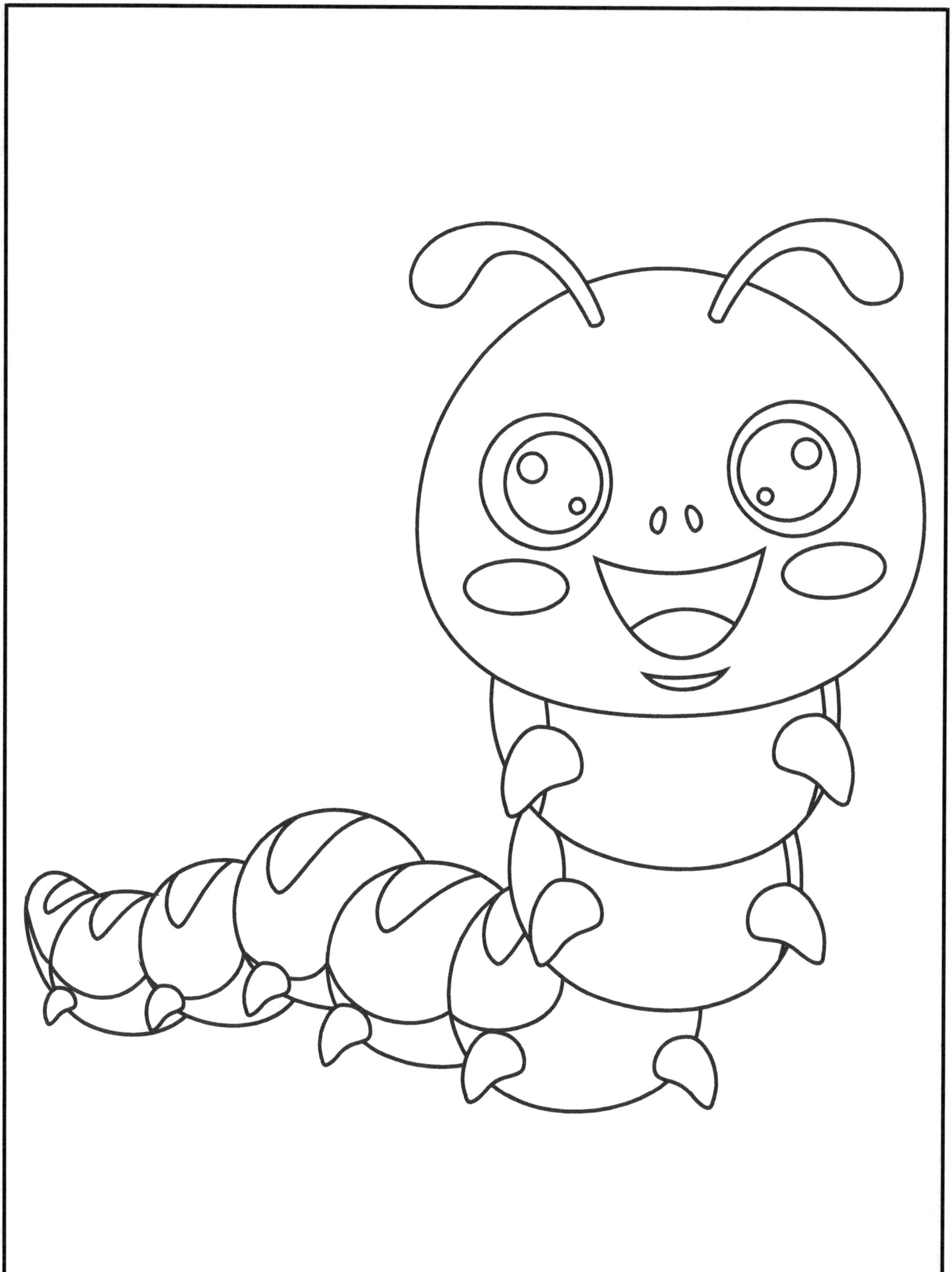

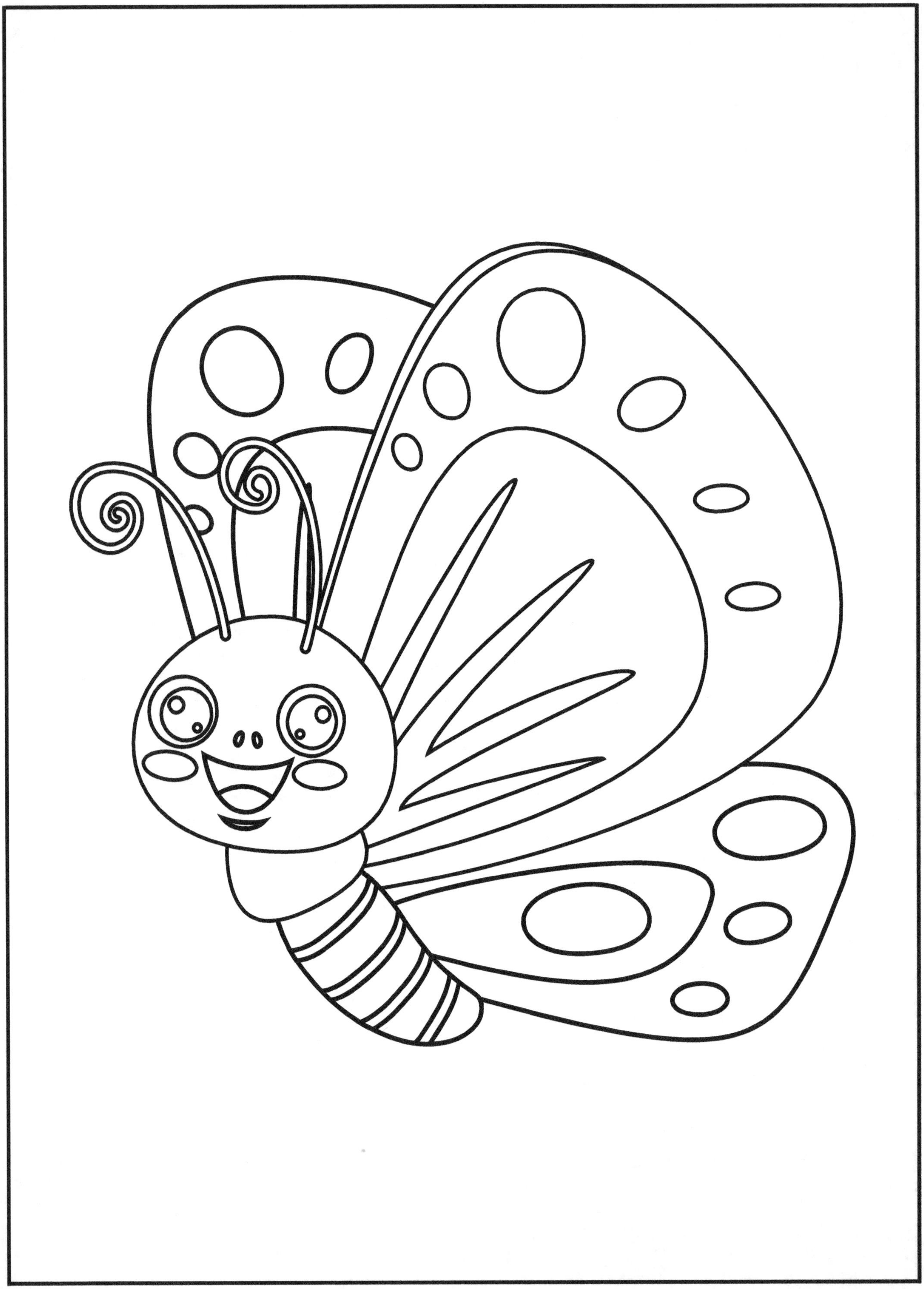

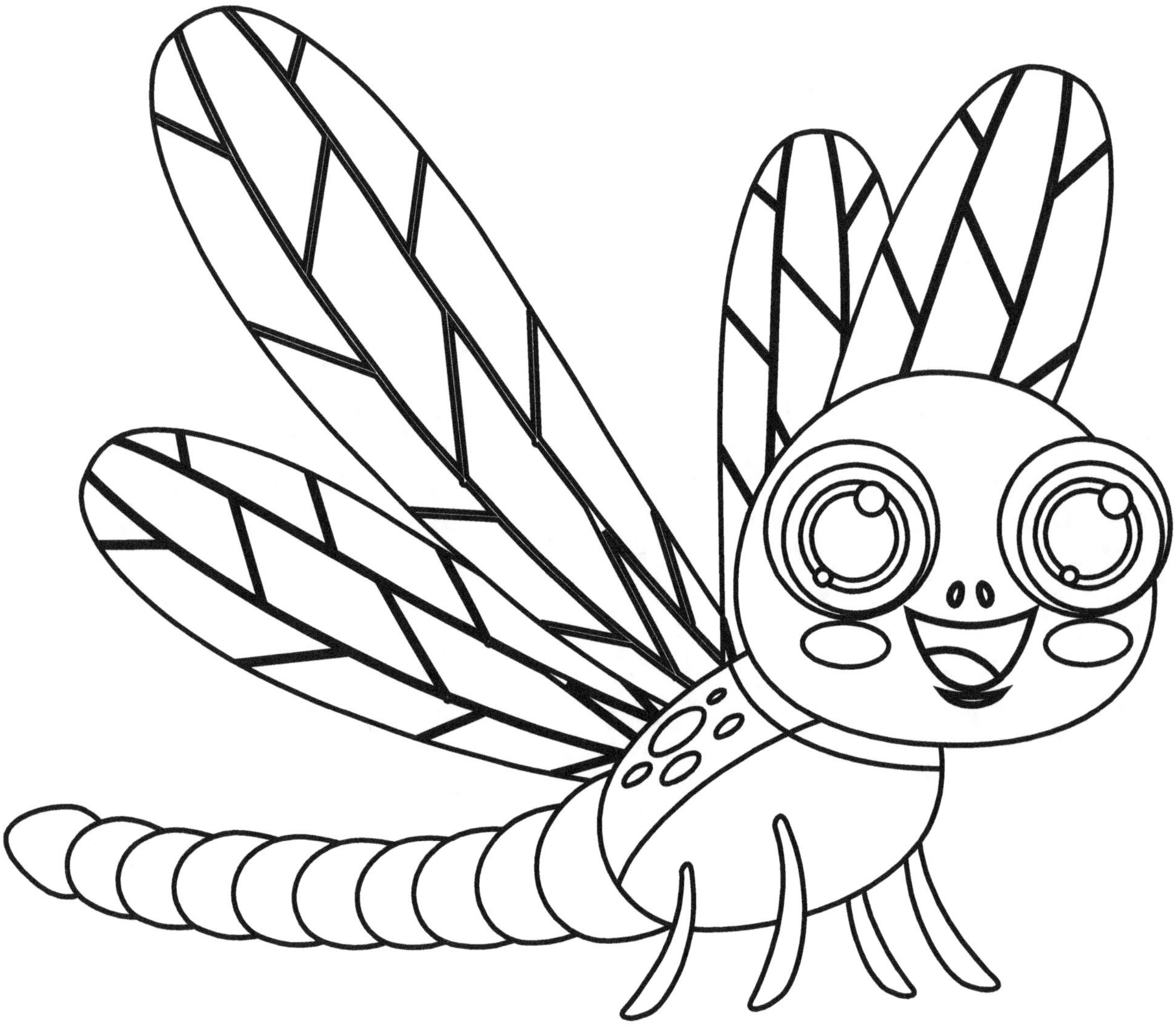

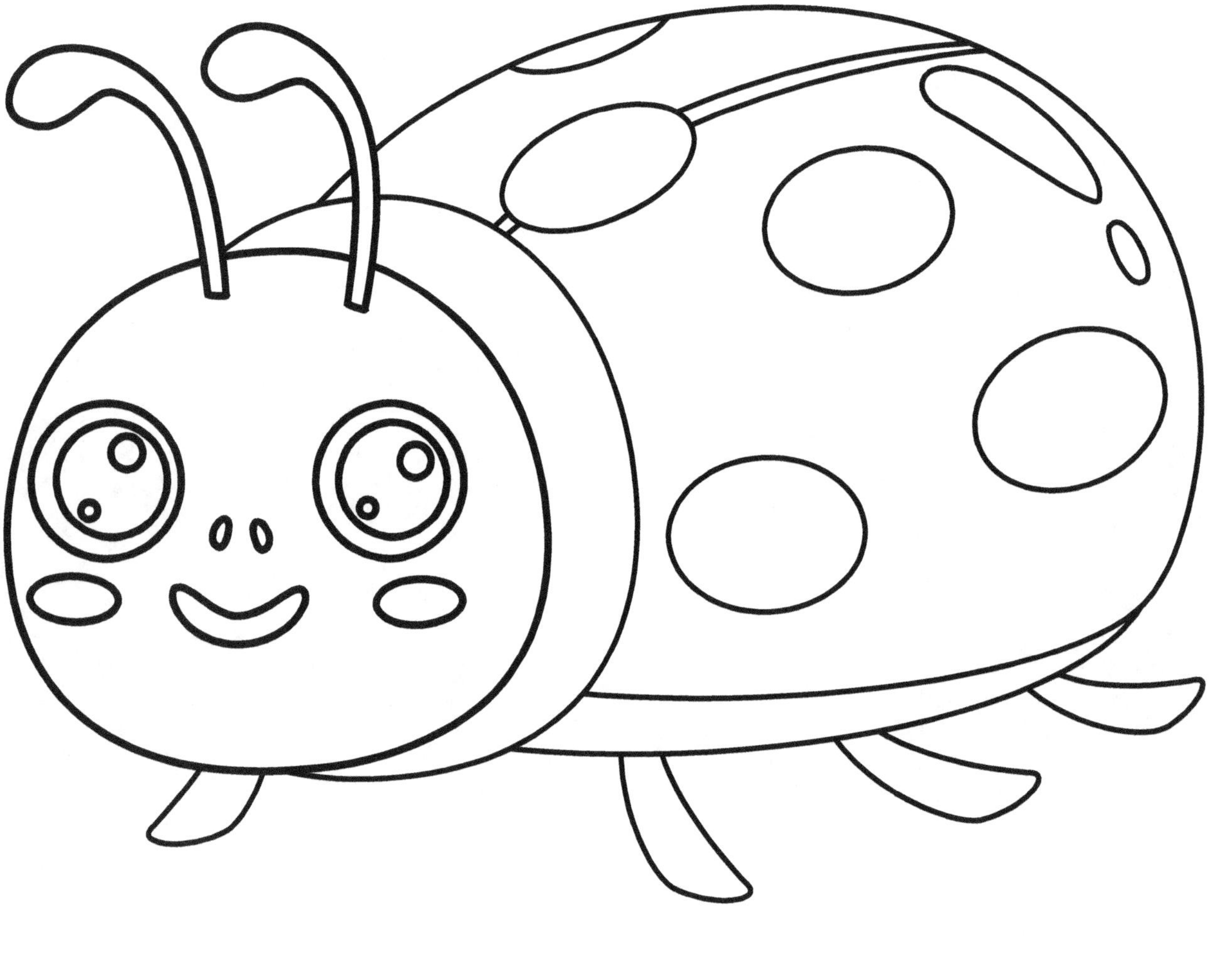

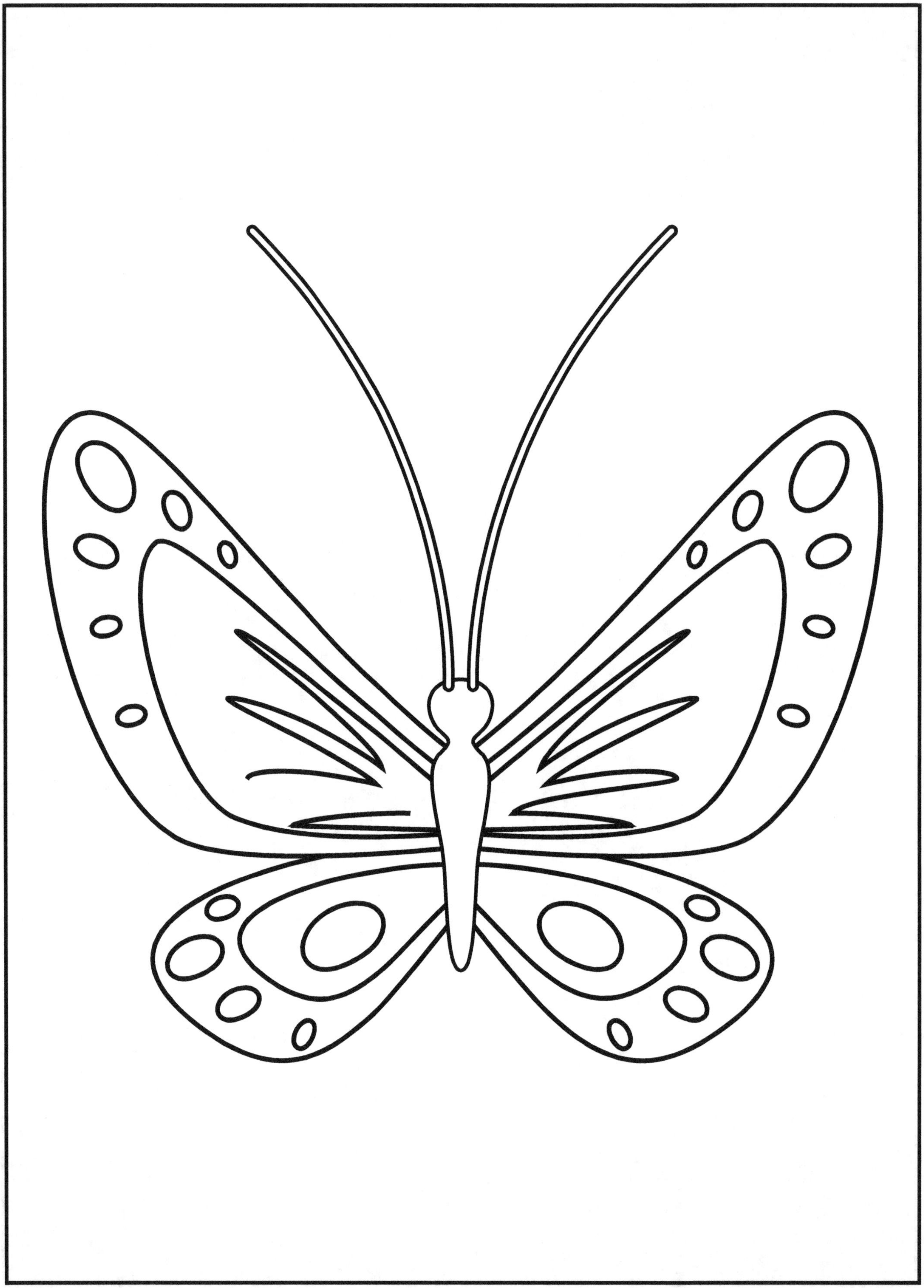

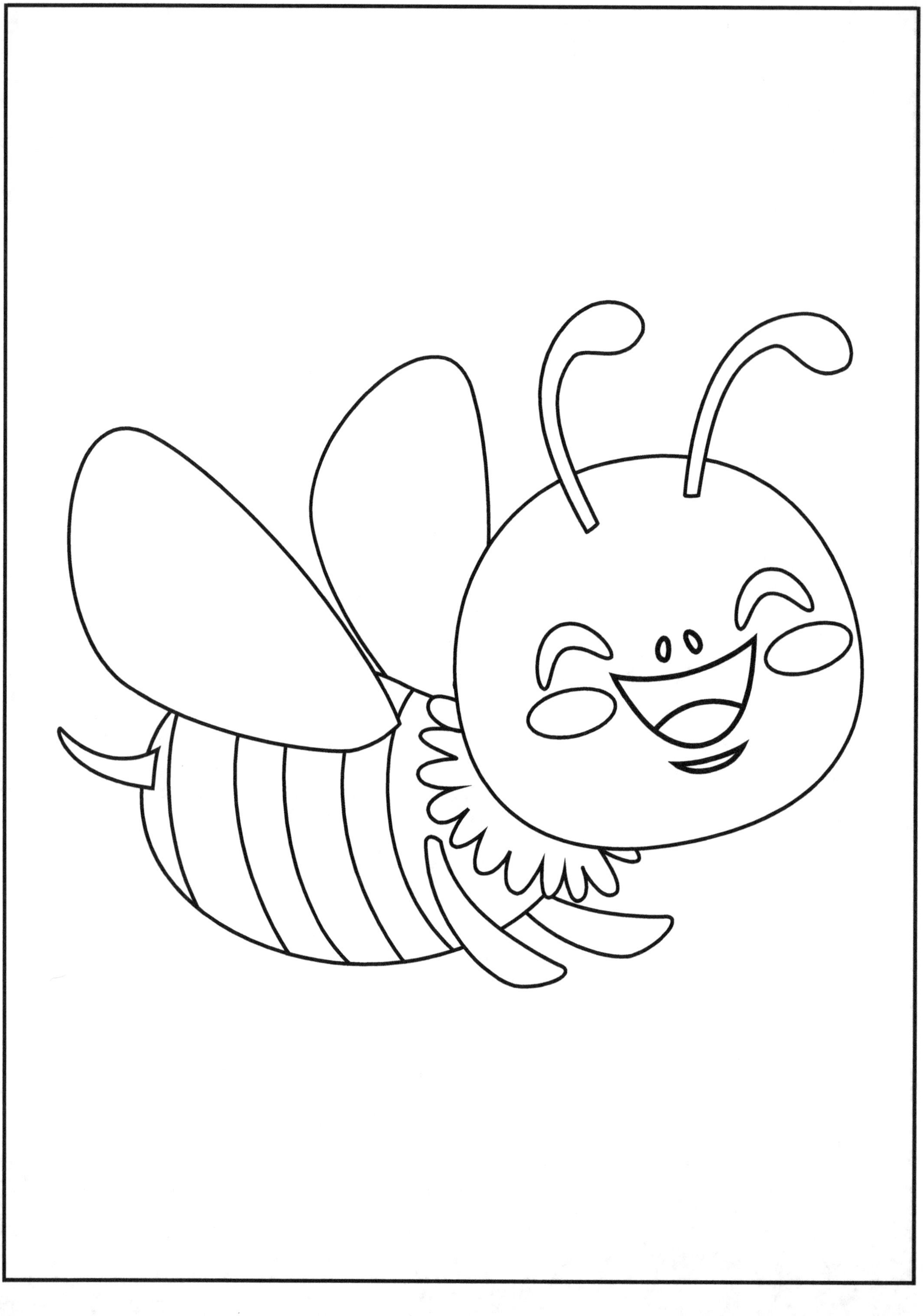

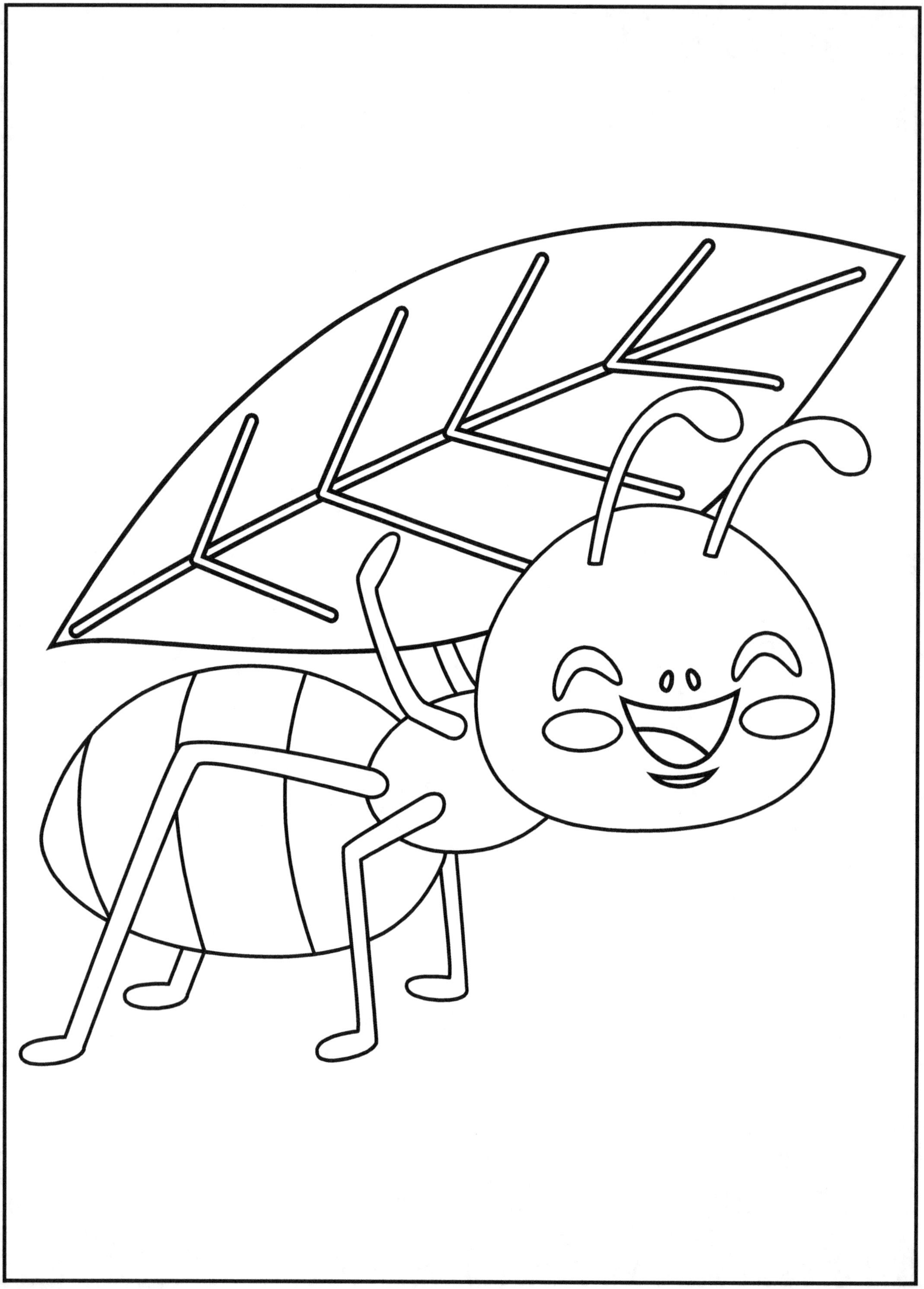

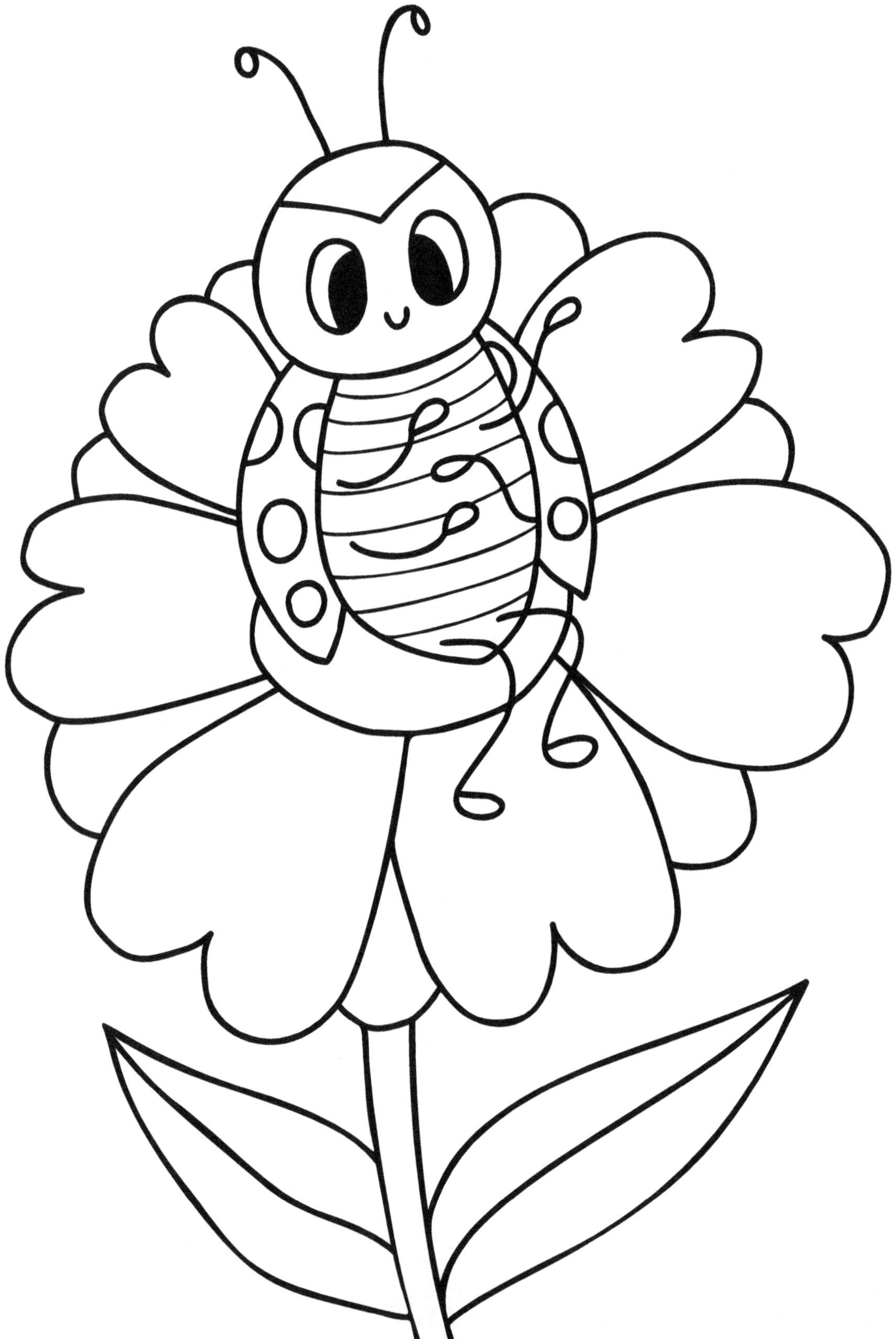

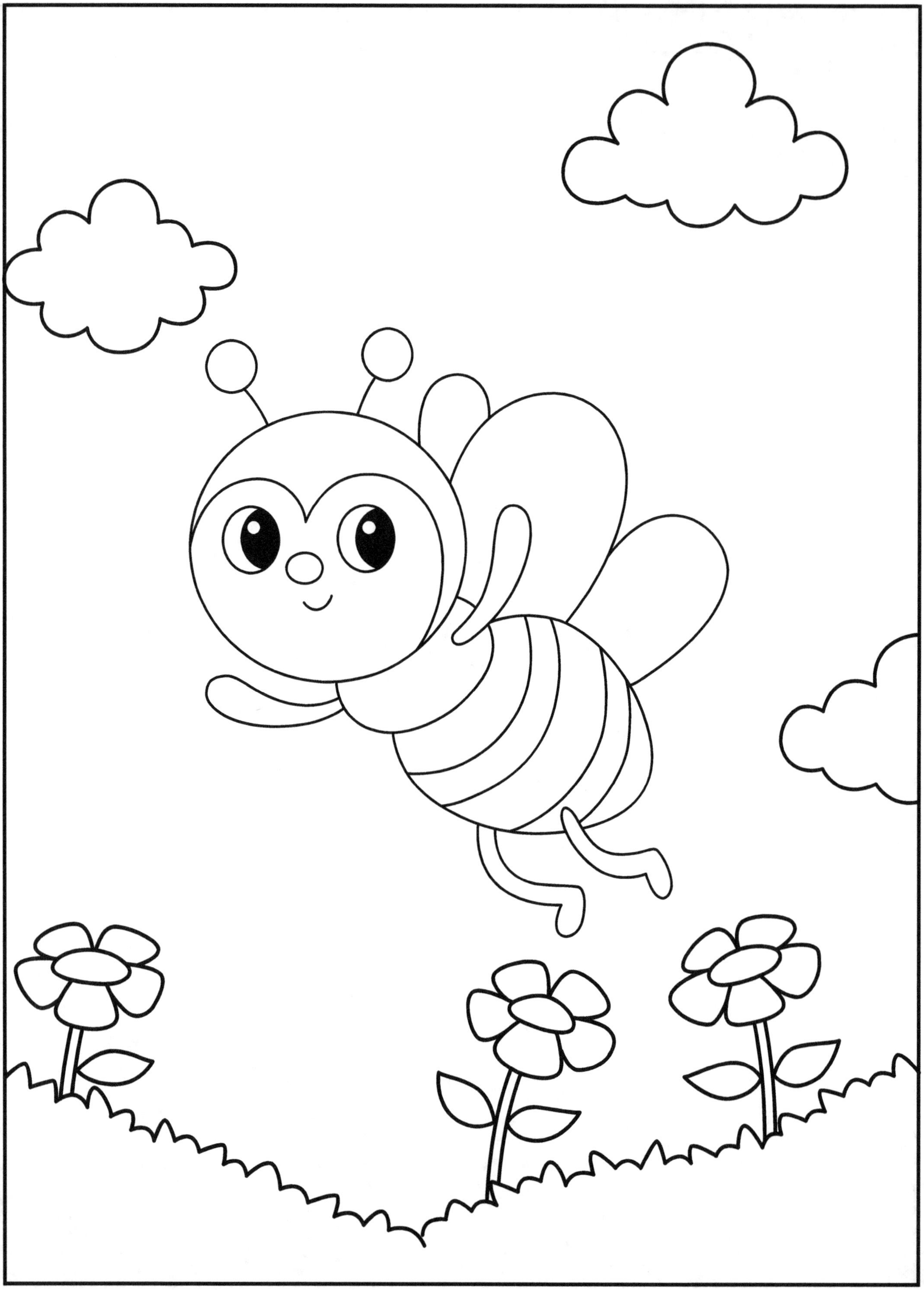

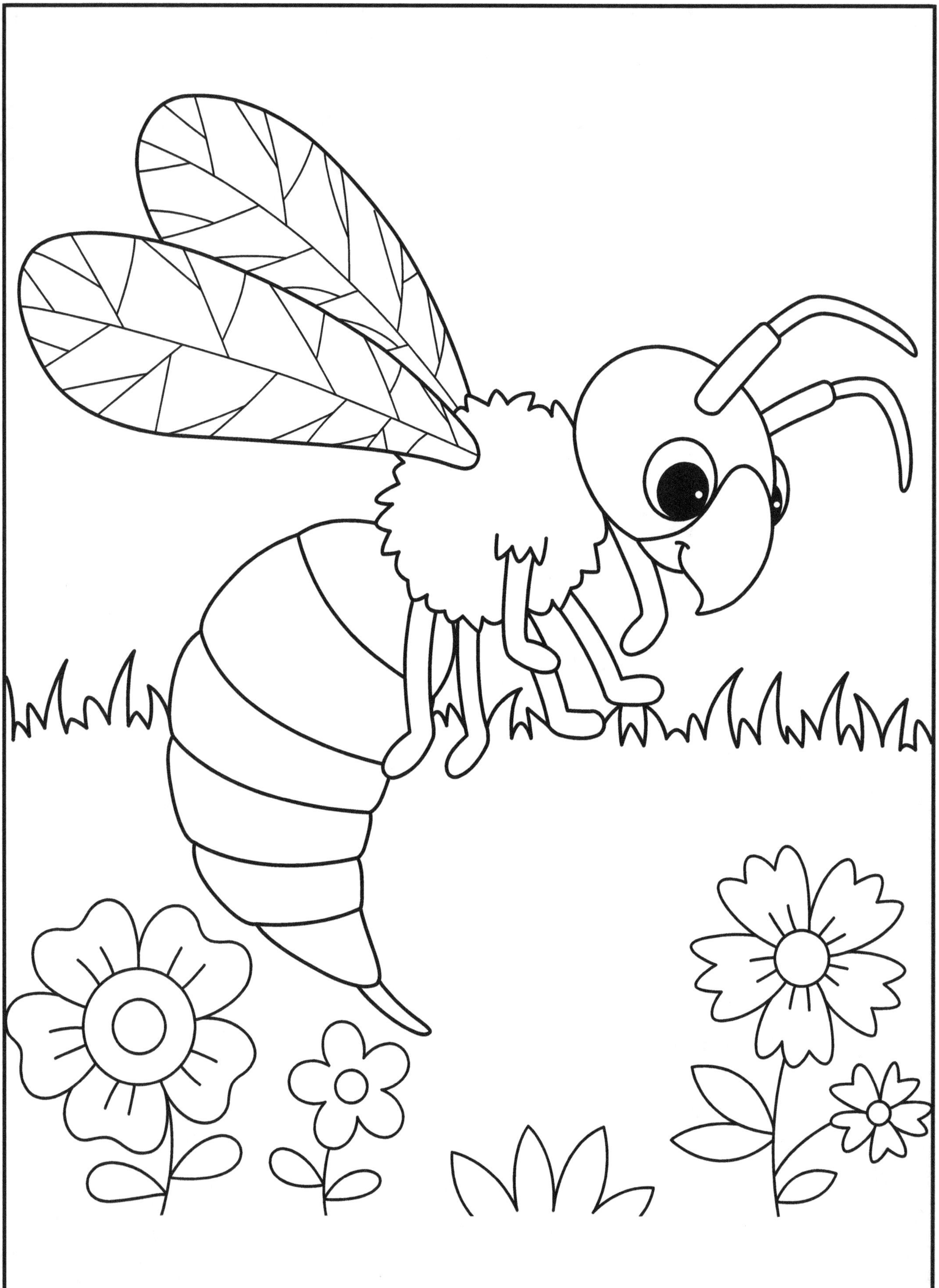

Zoo
Animals

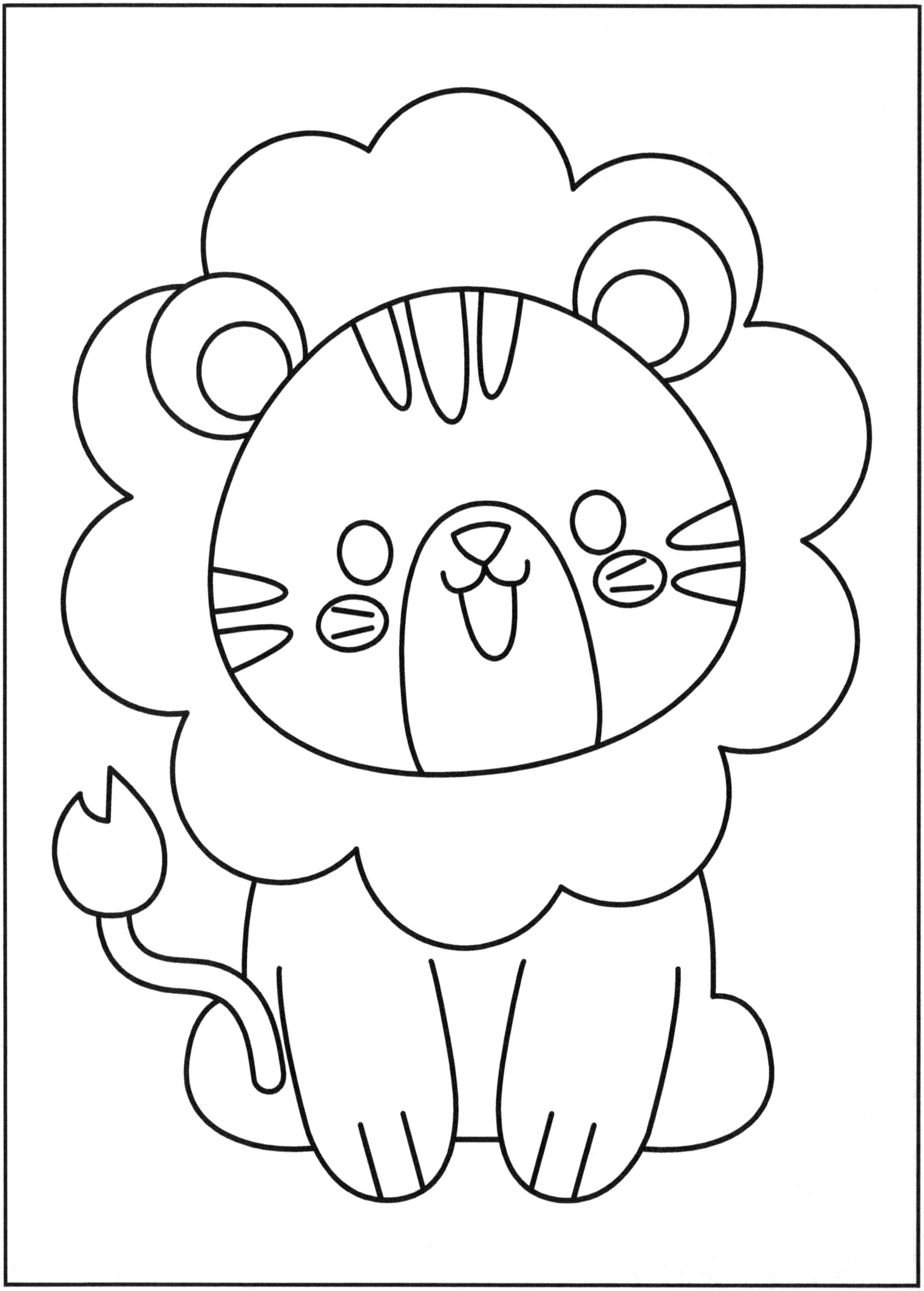

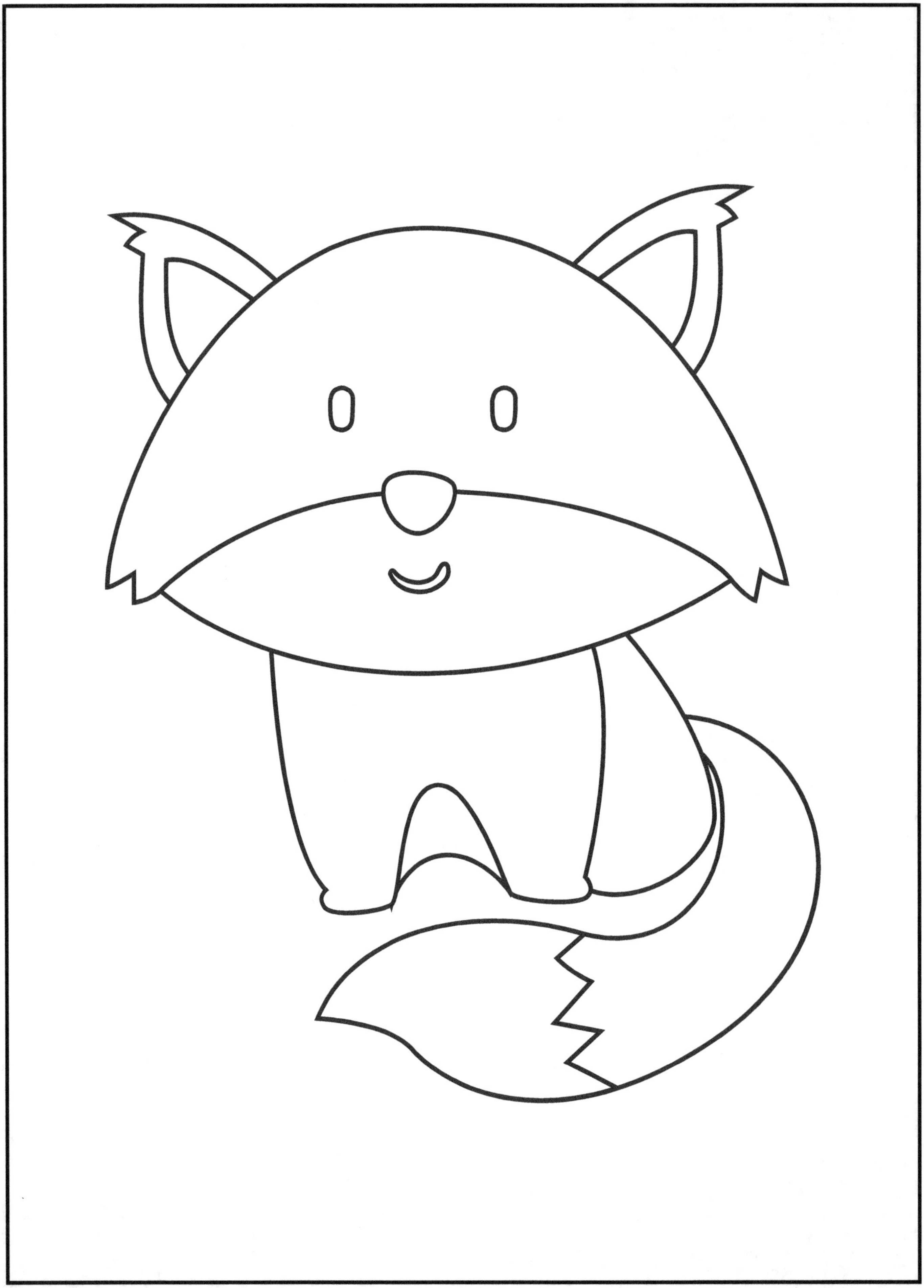

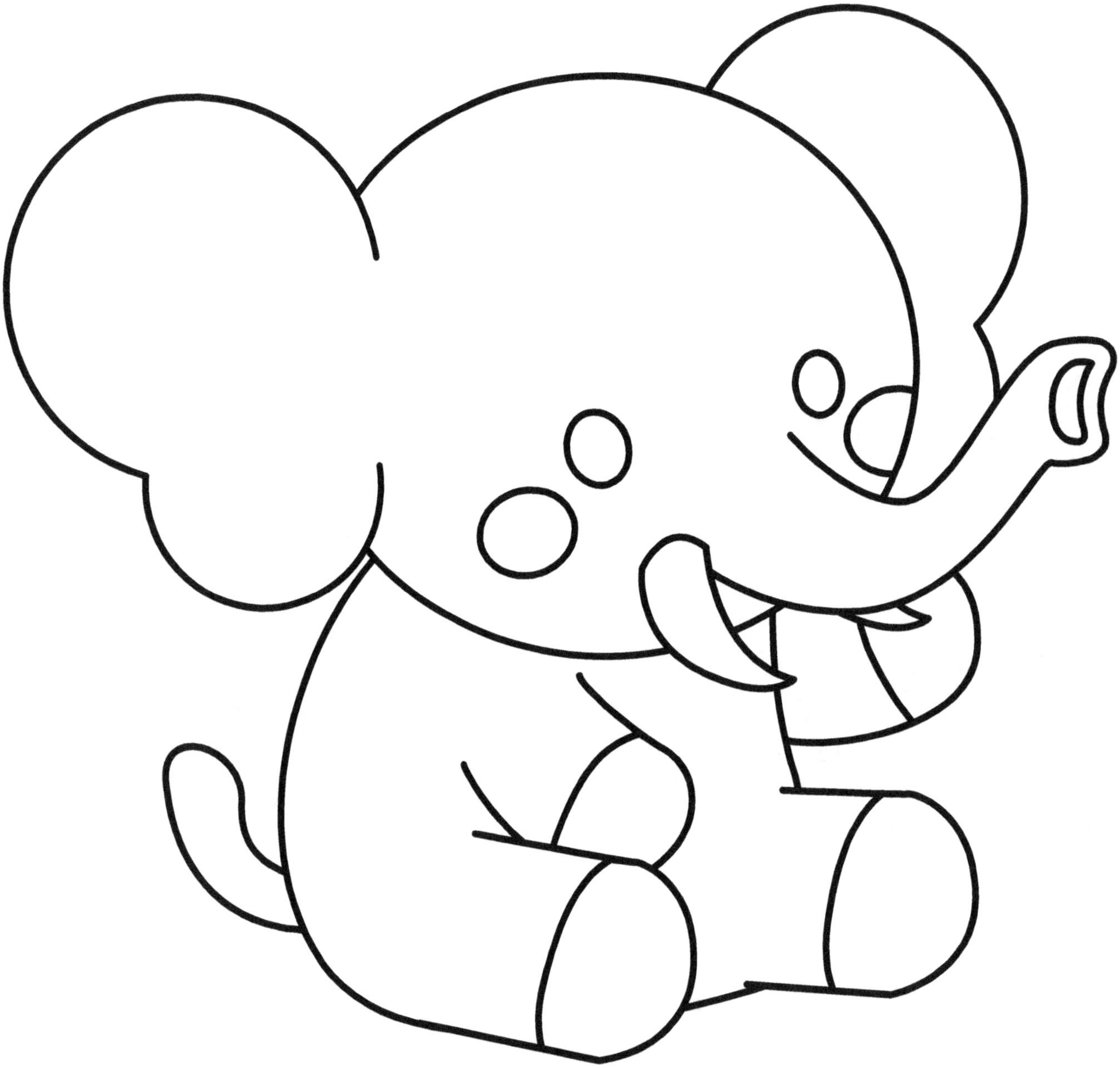

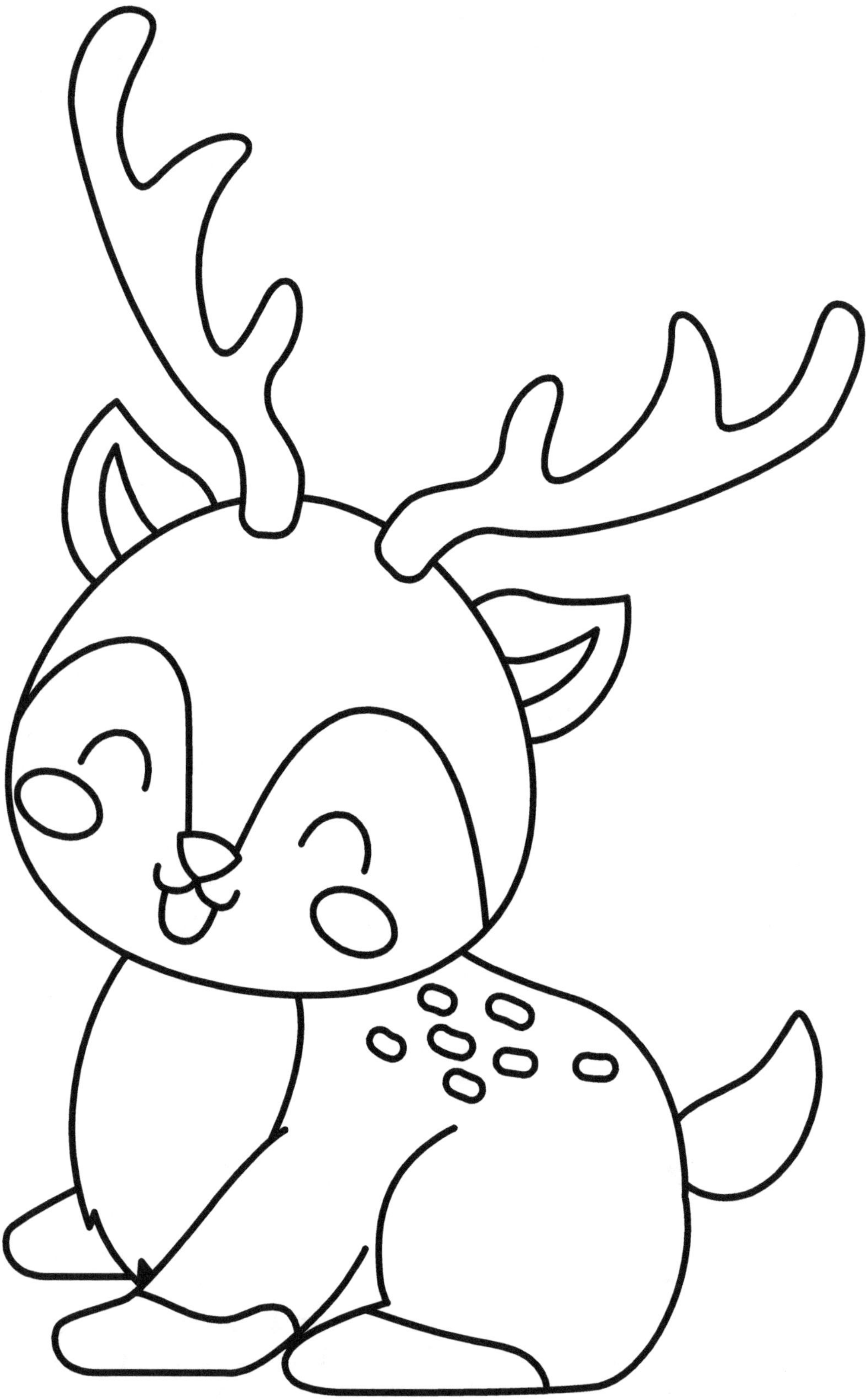

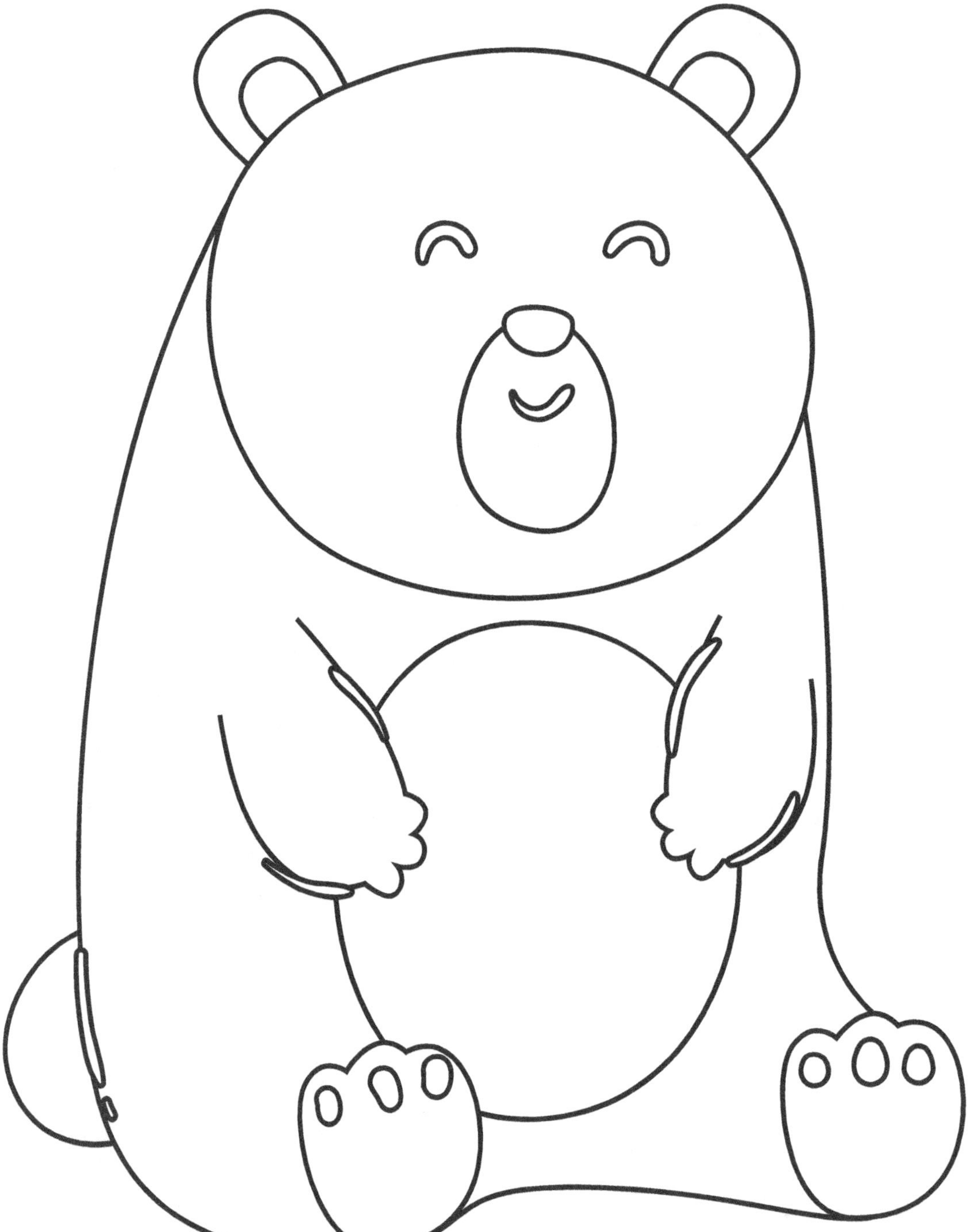

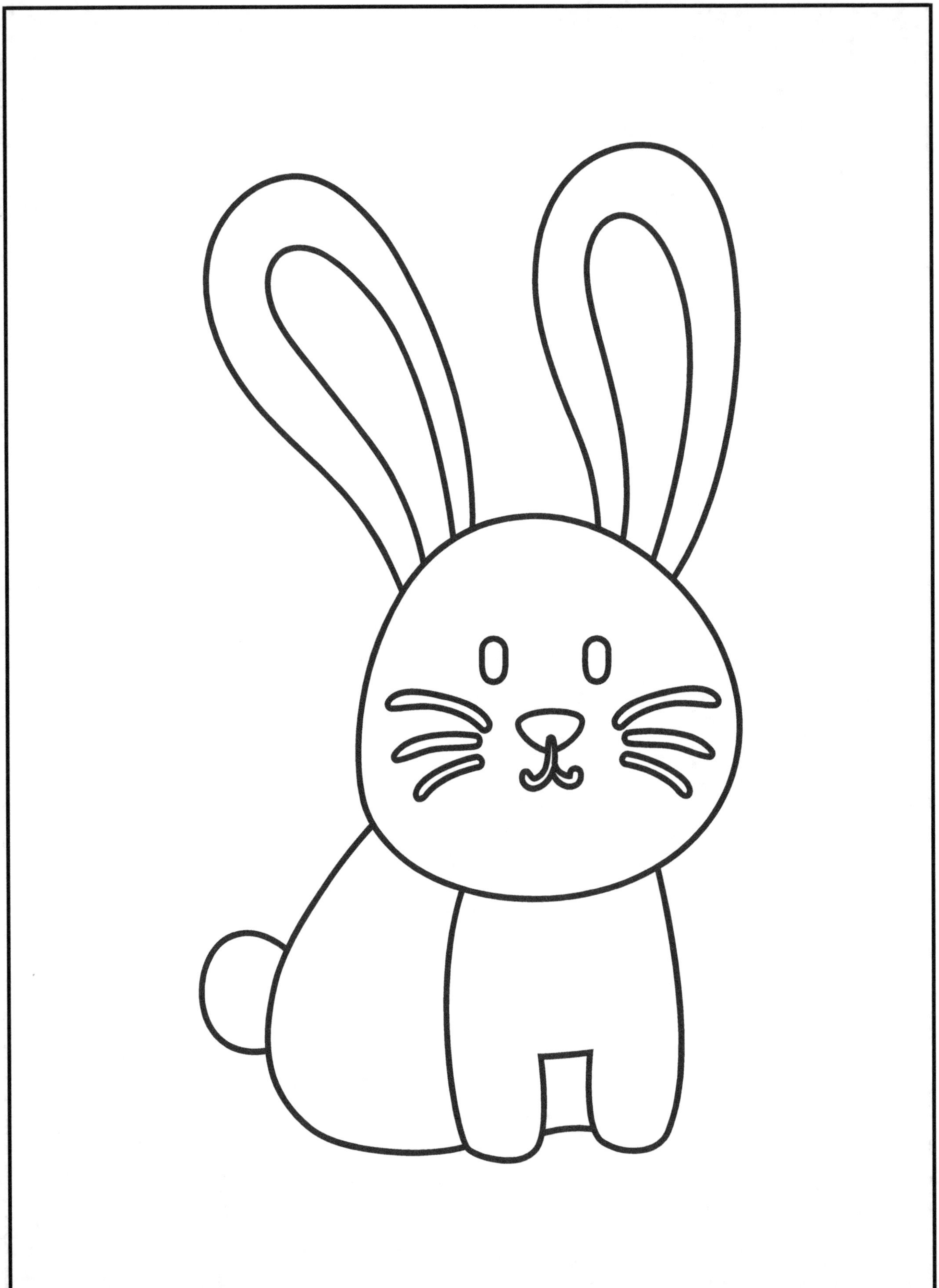

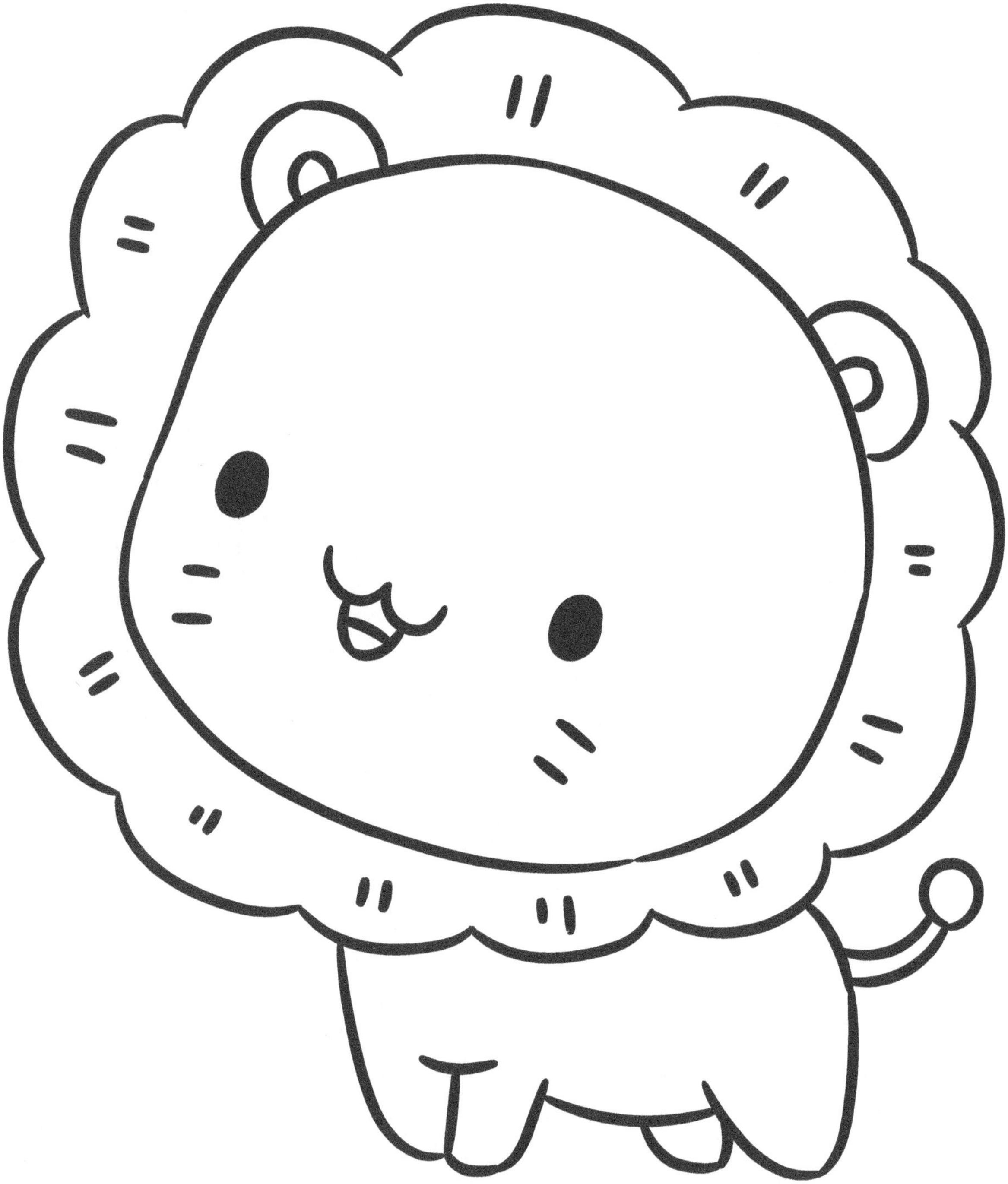

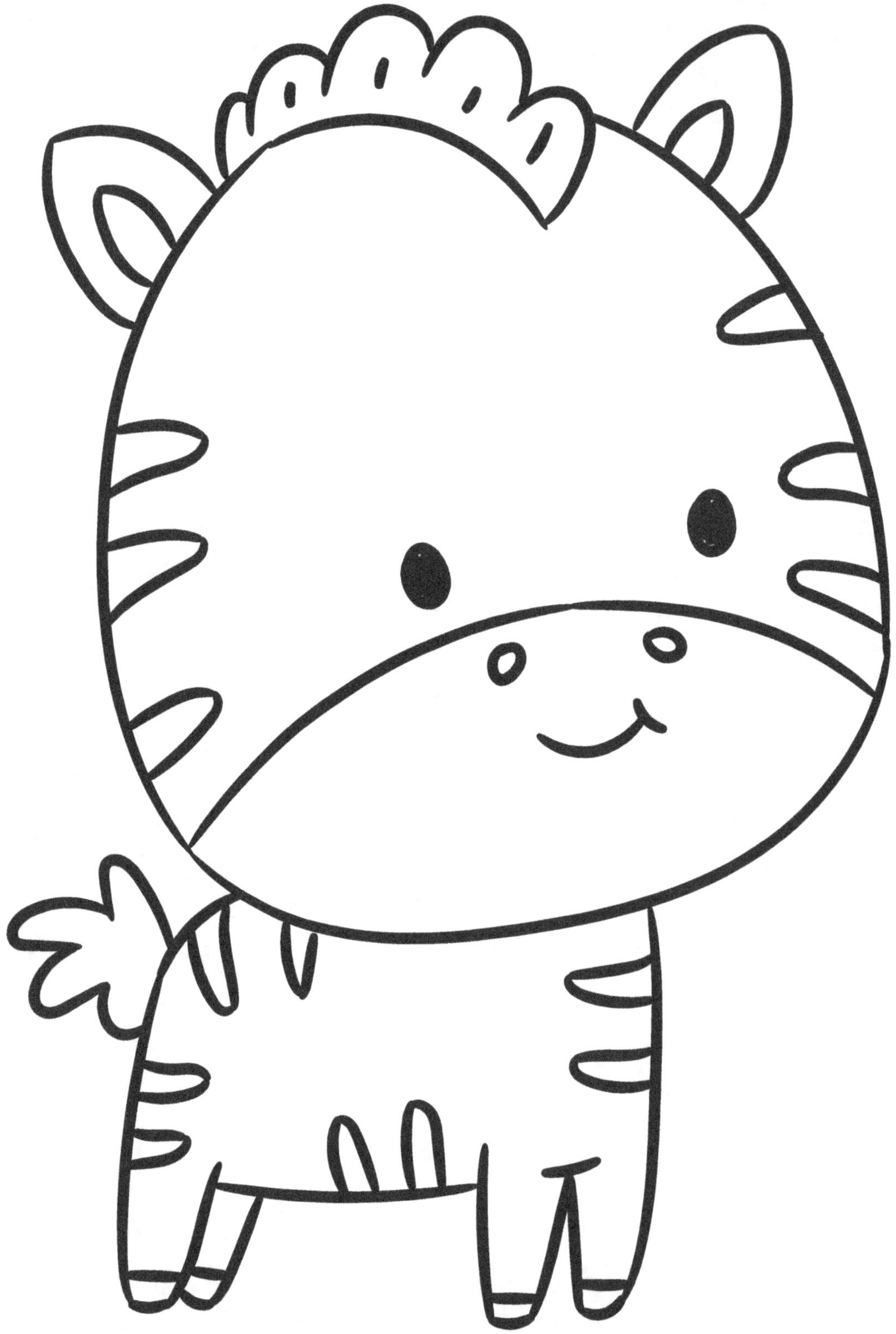

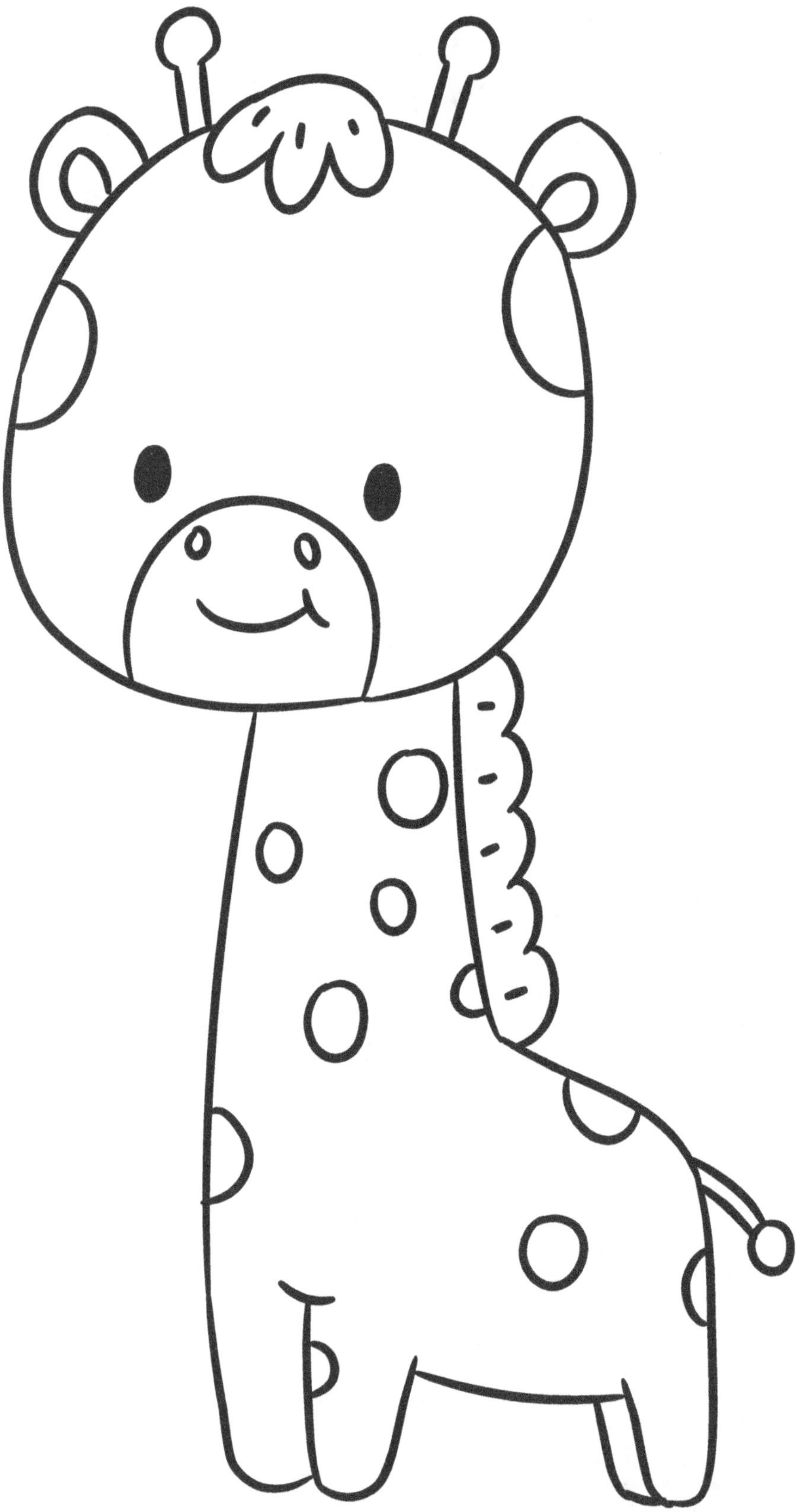

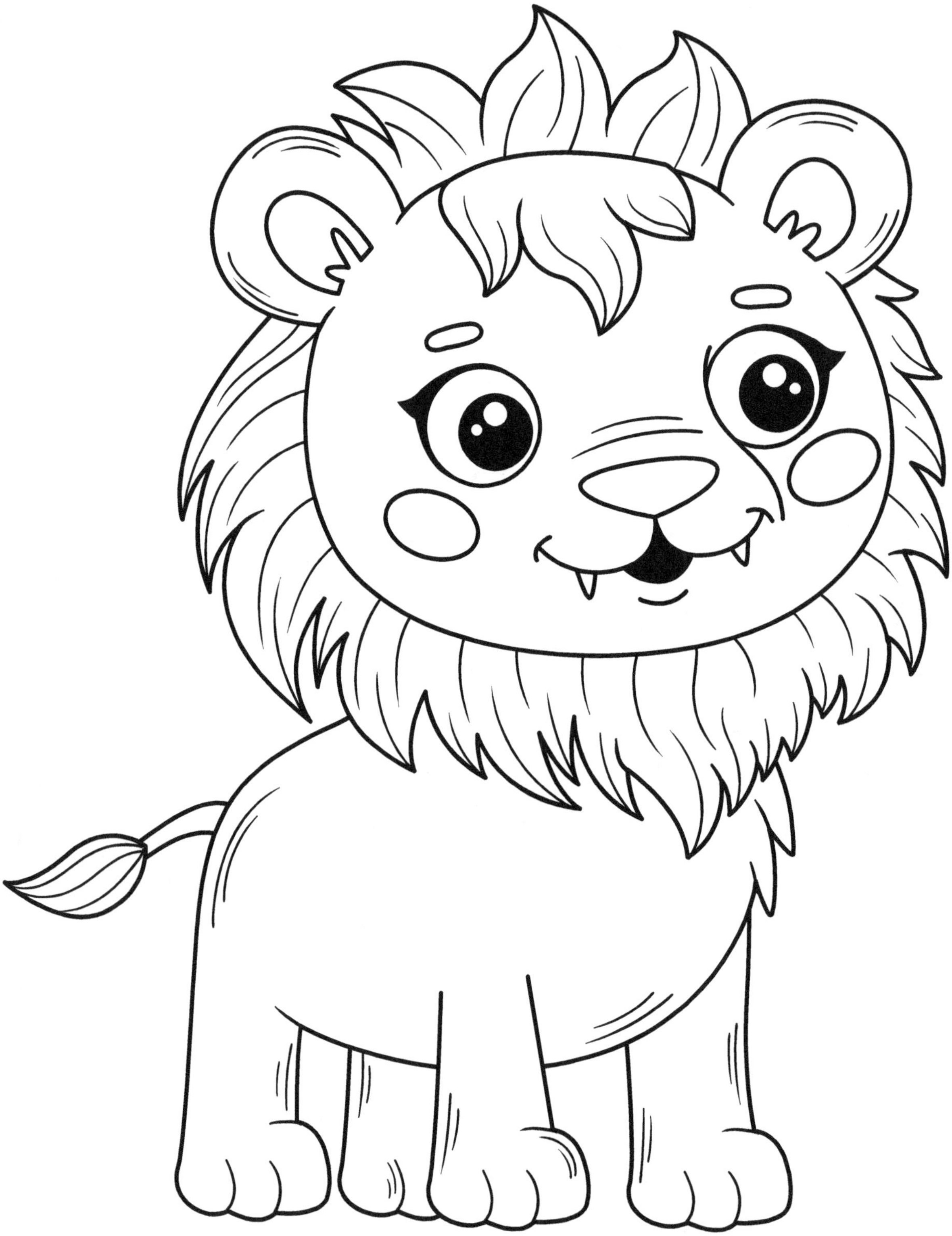

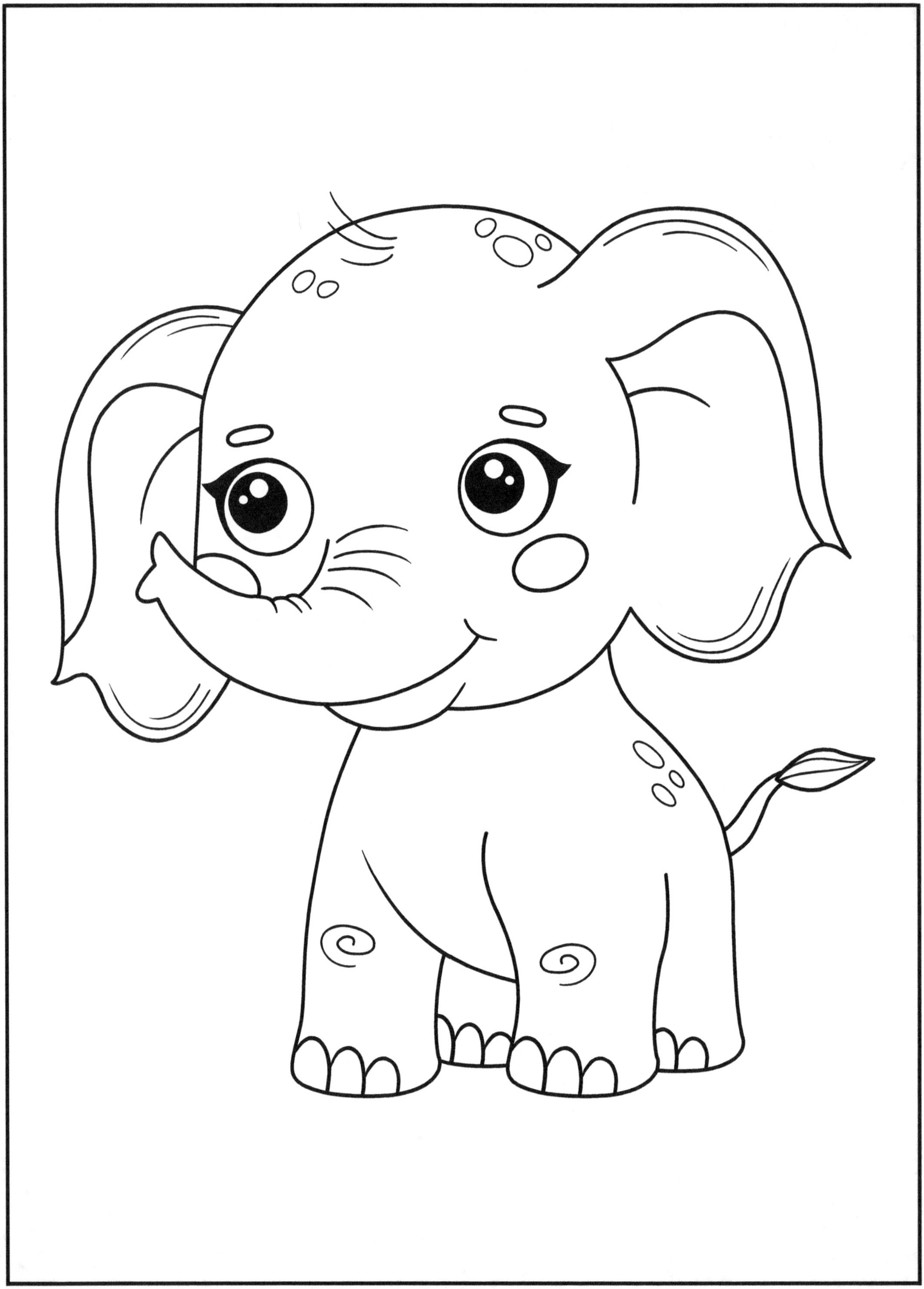

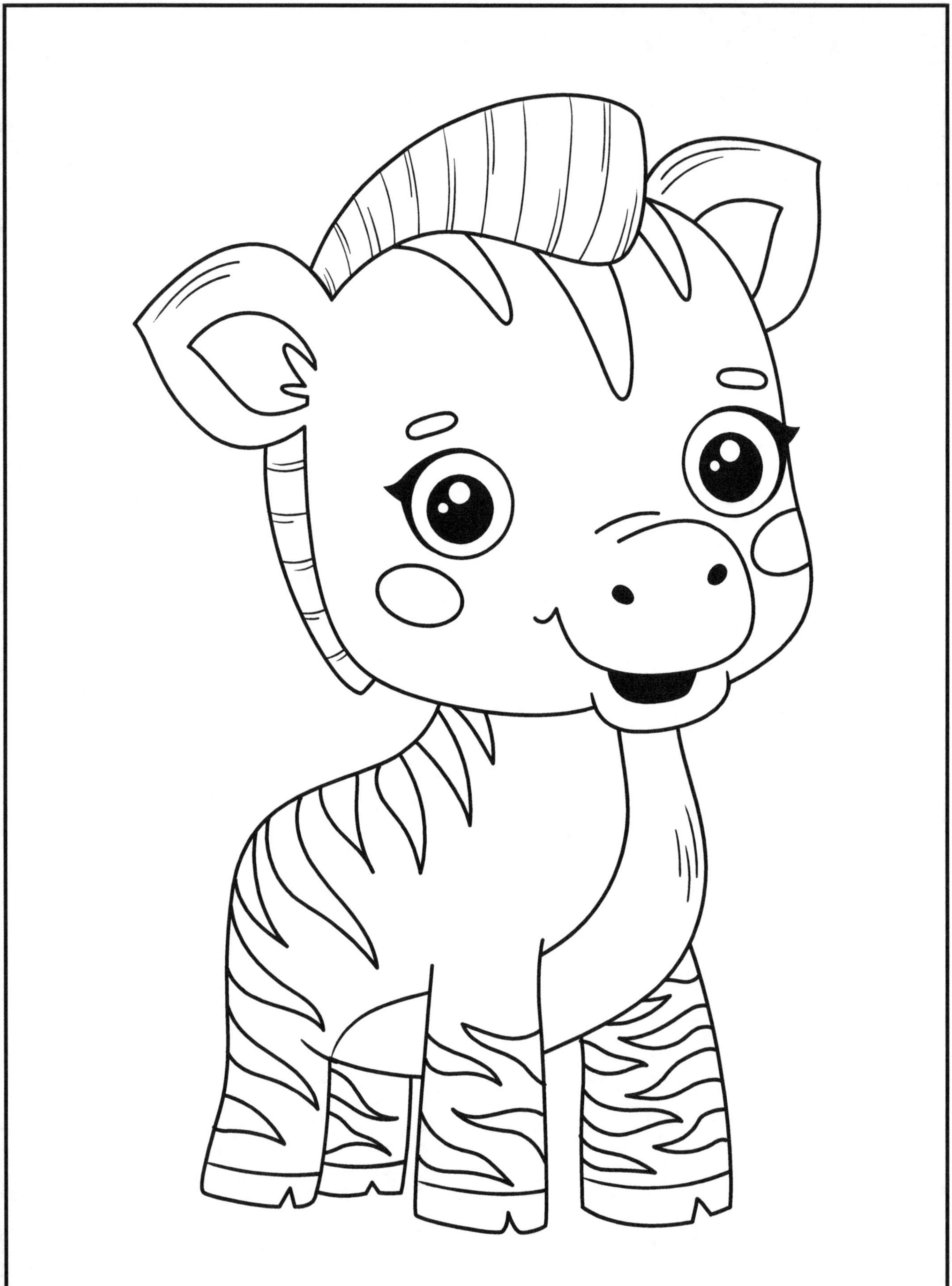

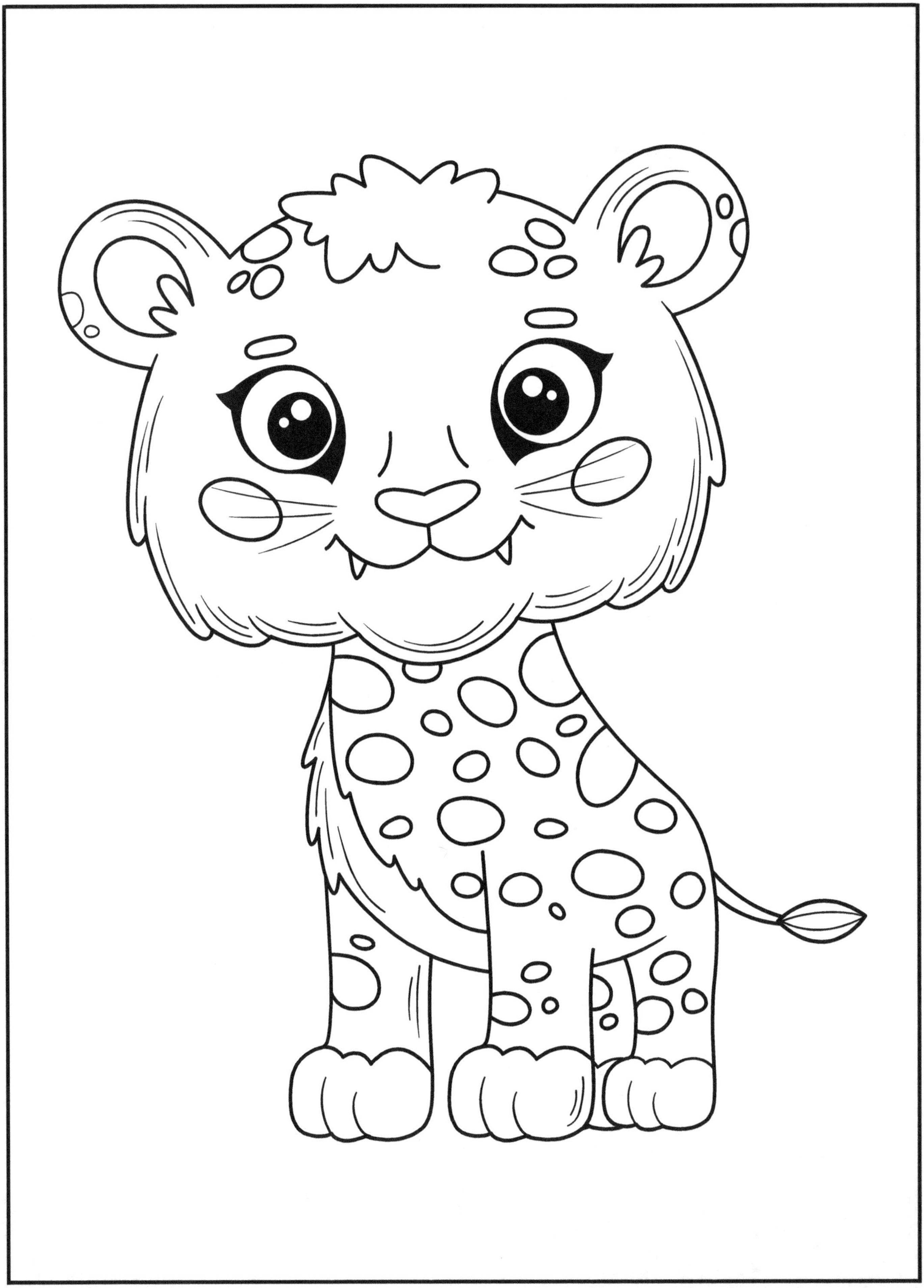

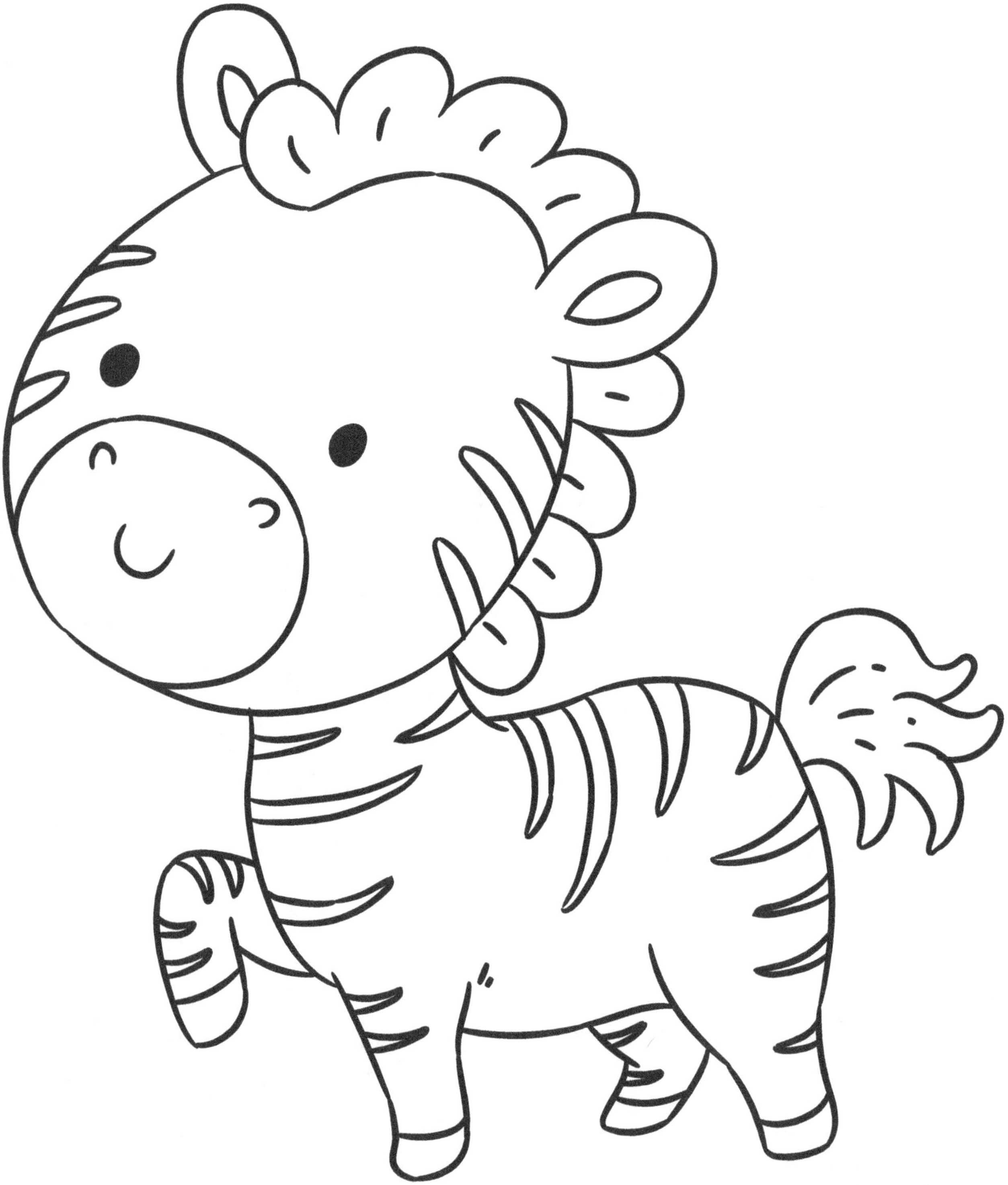

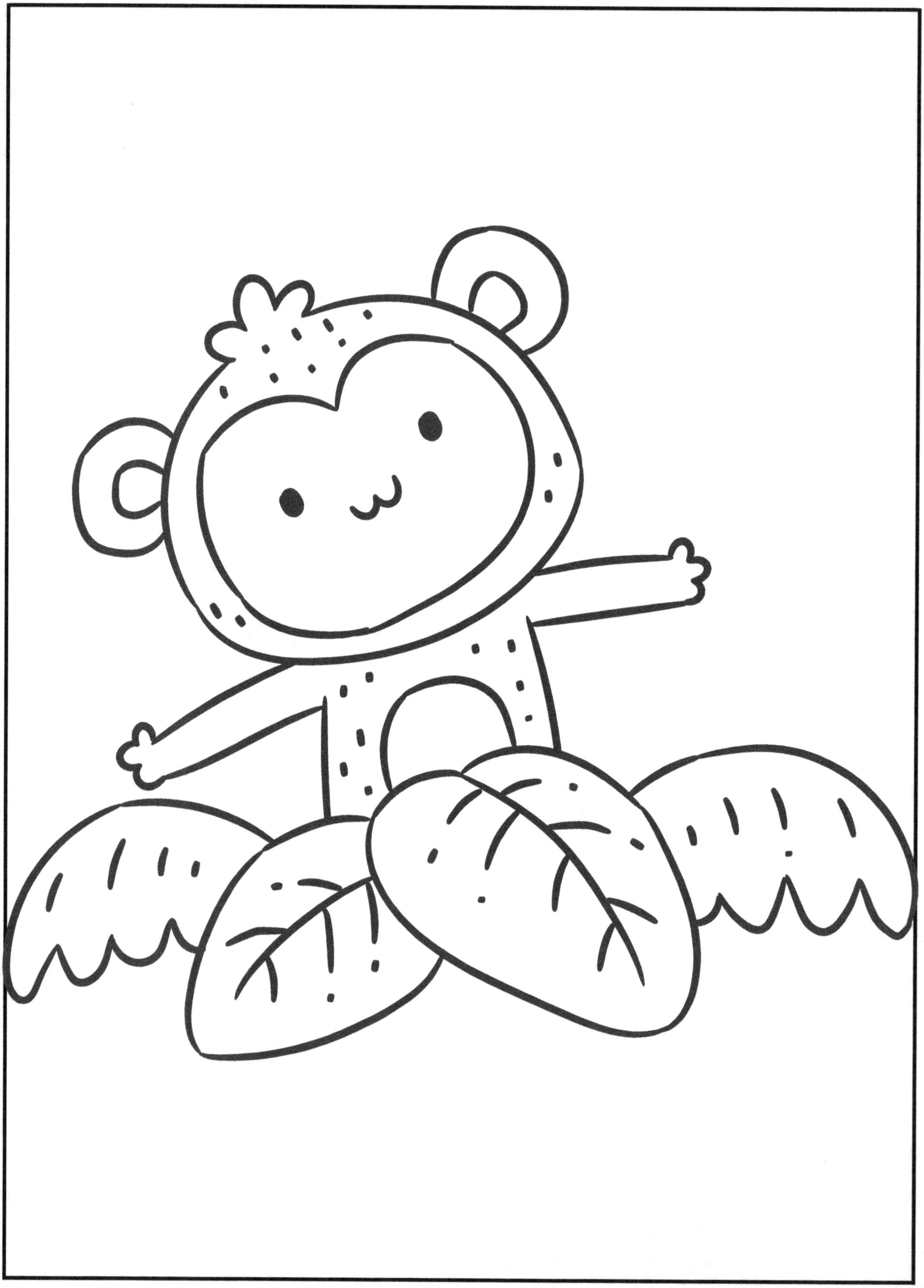

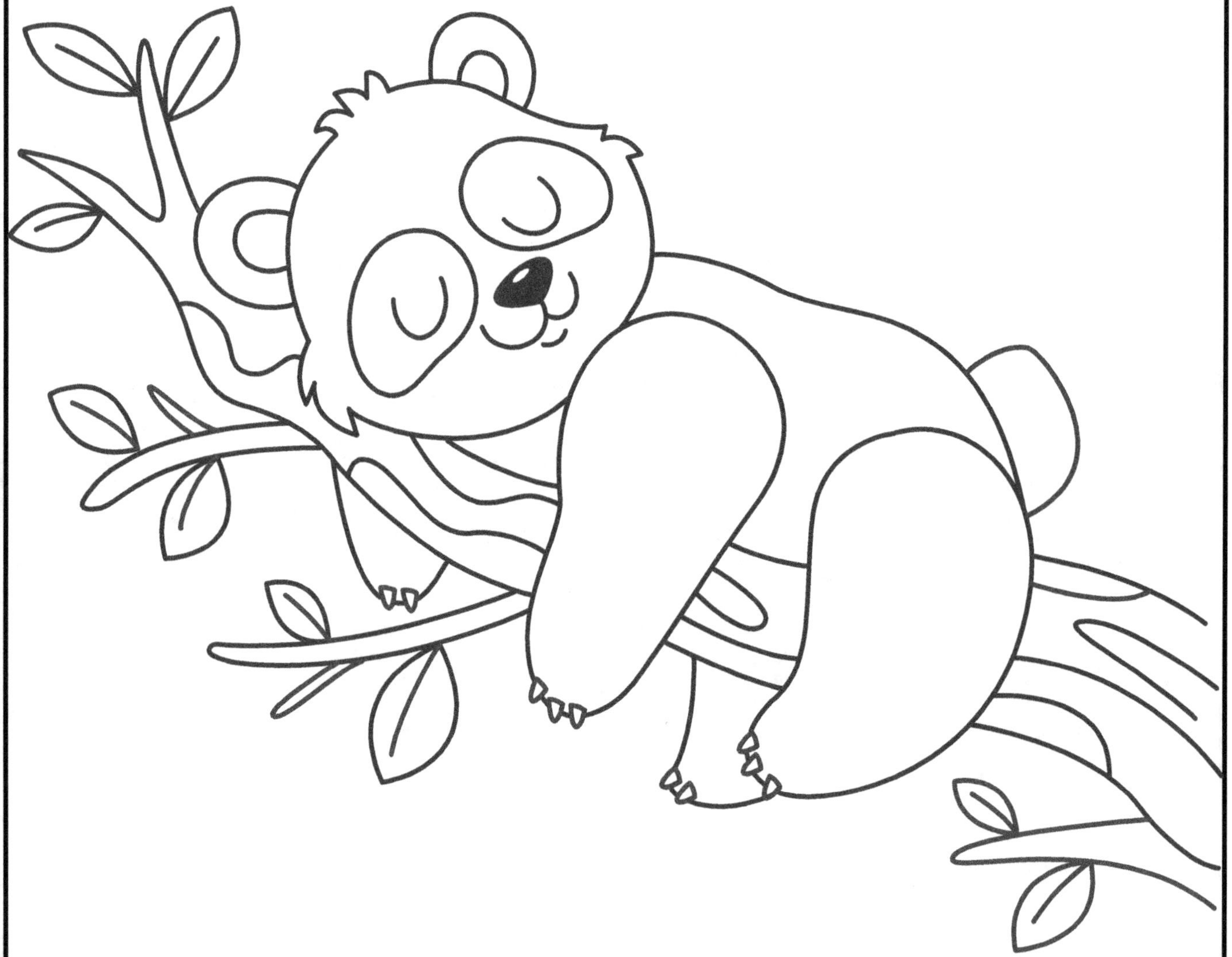

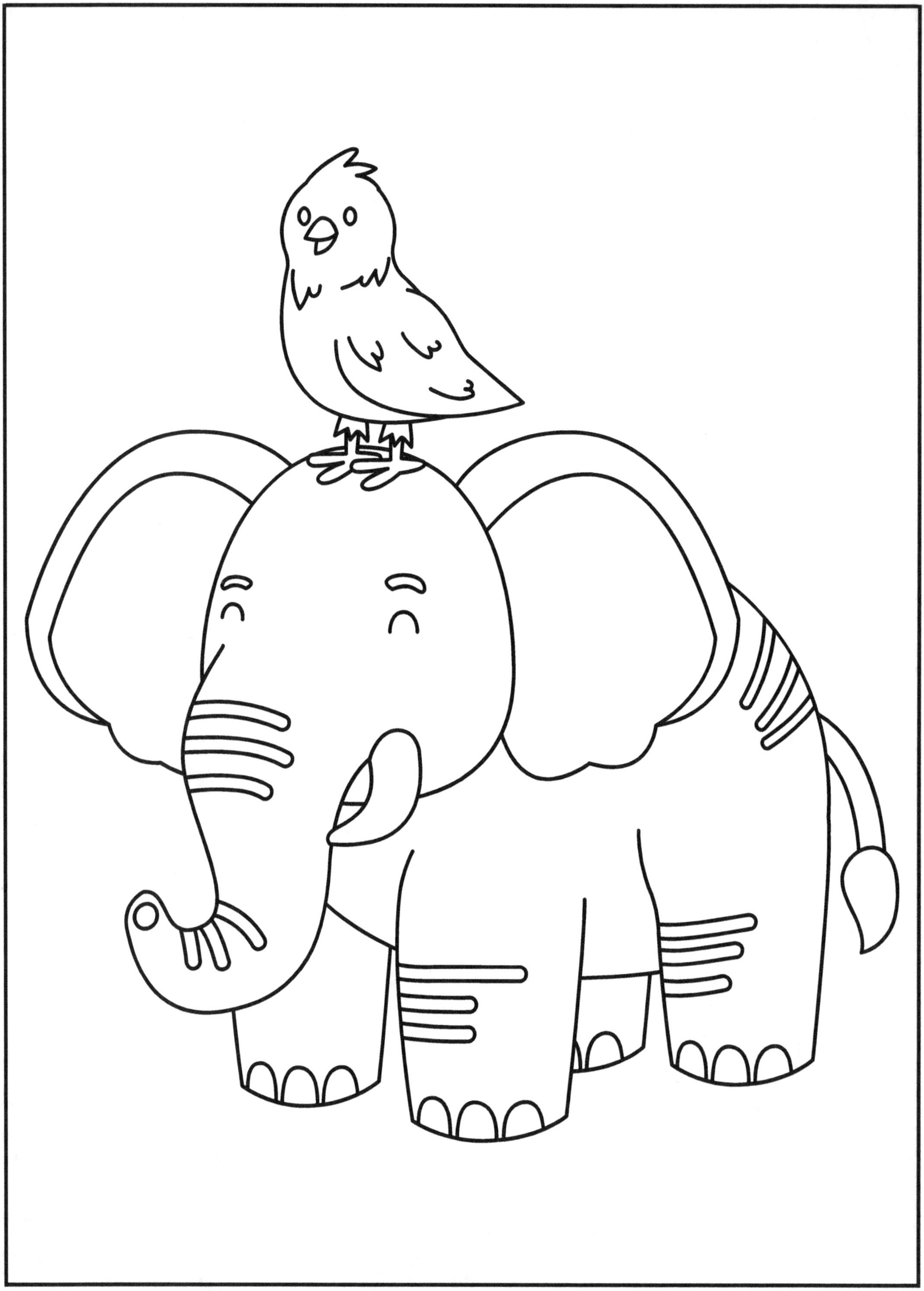

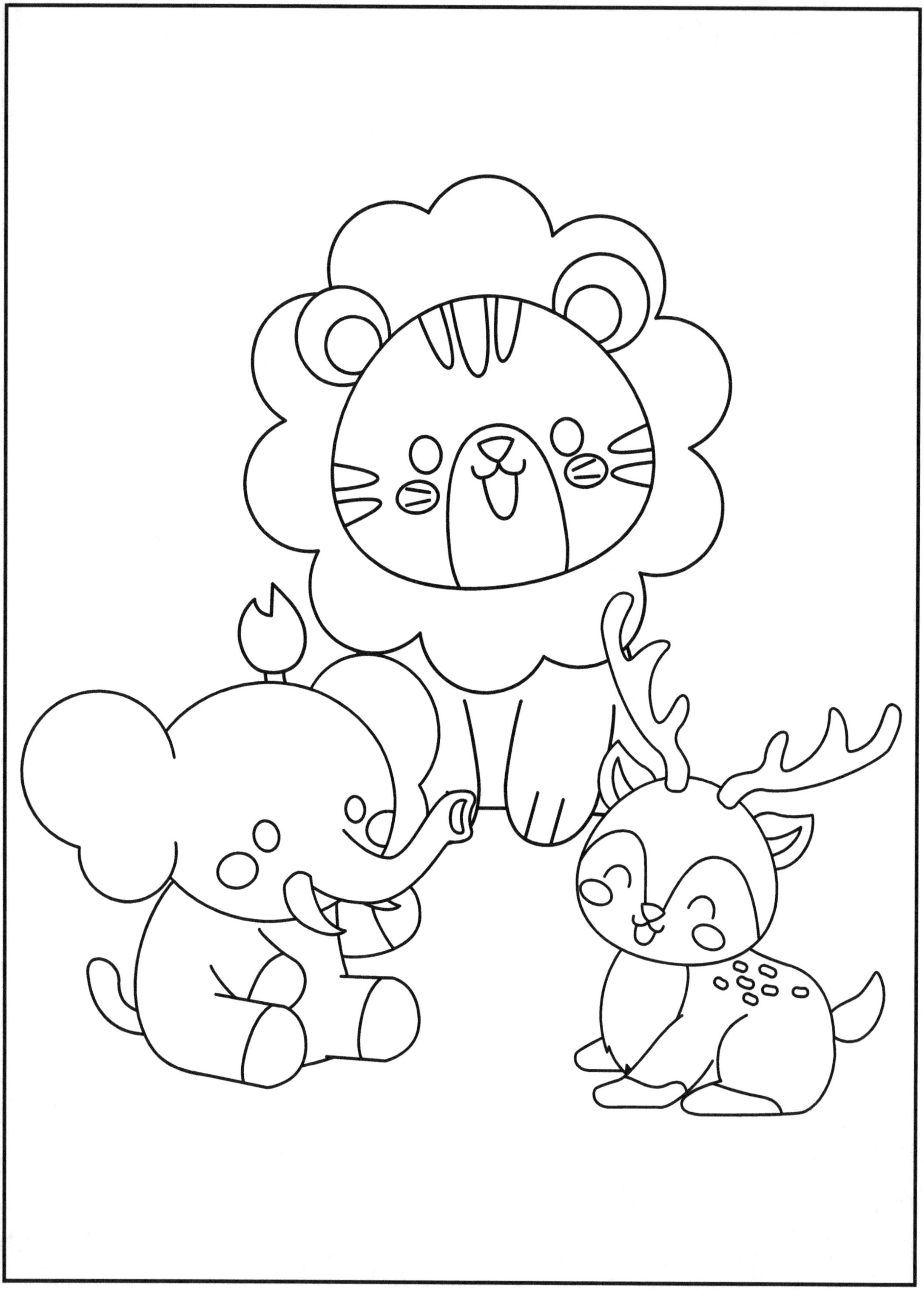

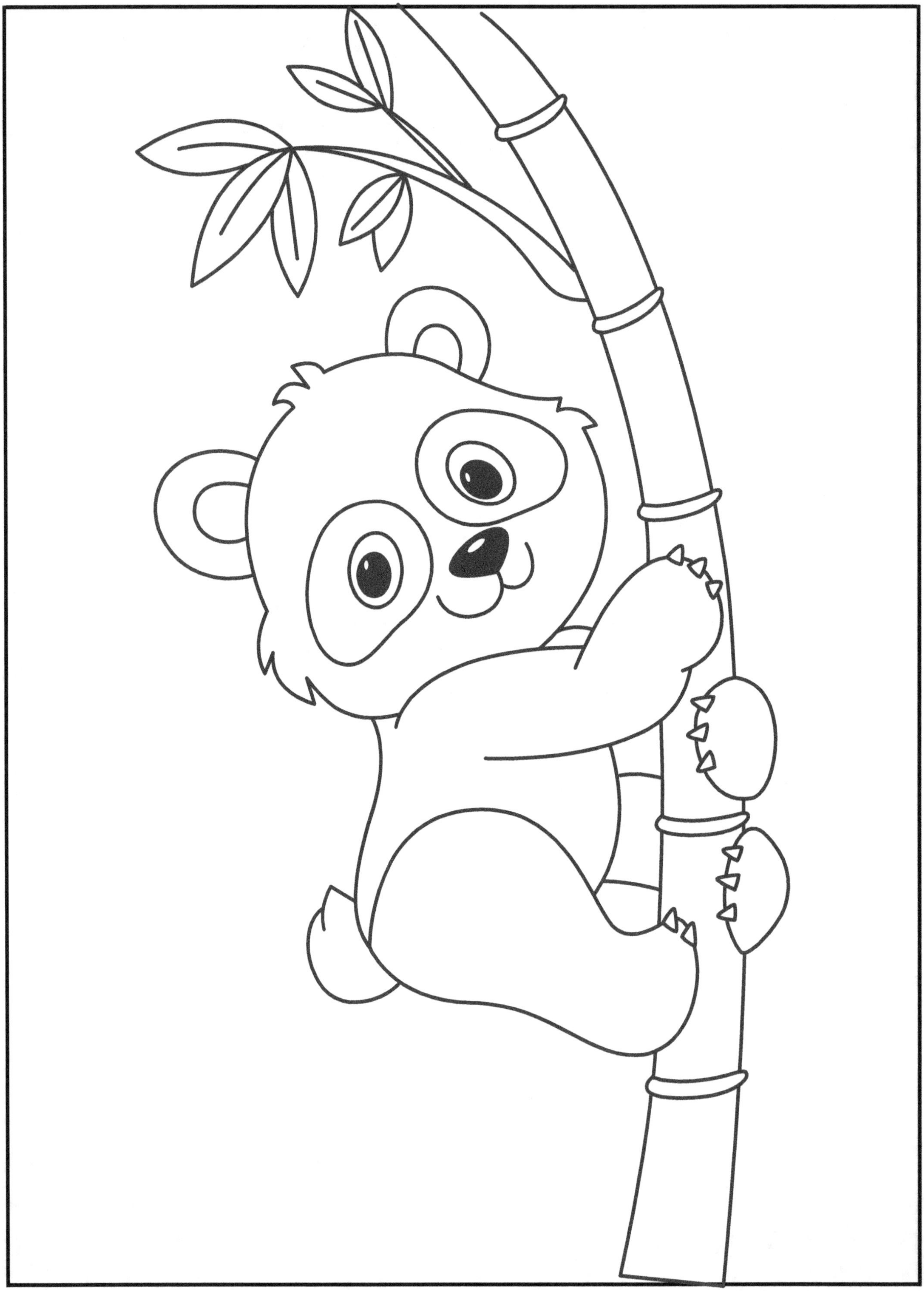

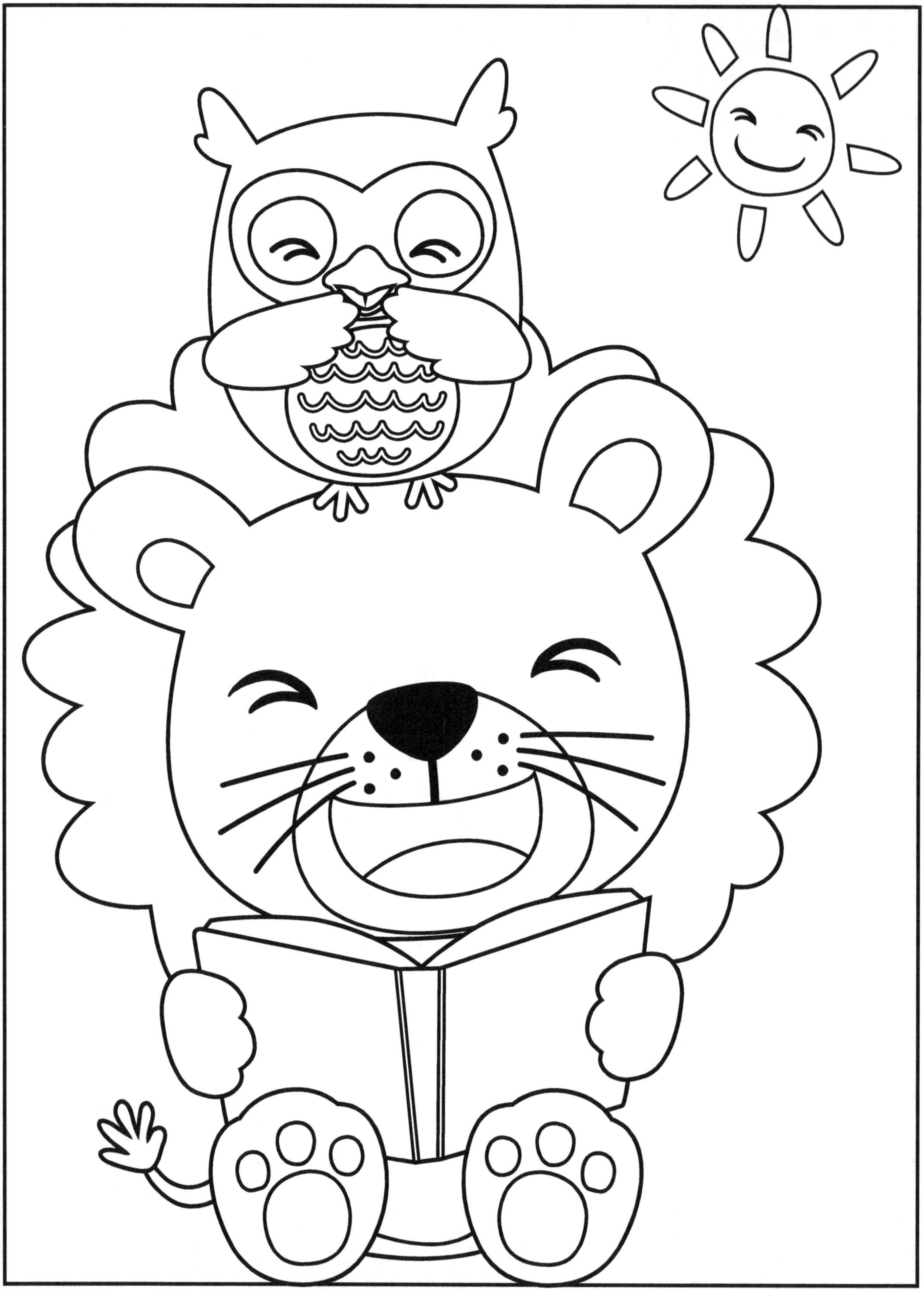

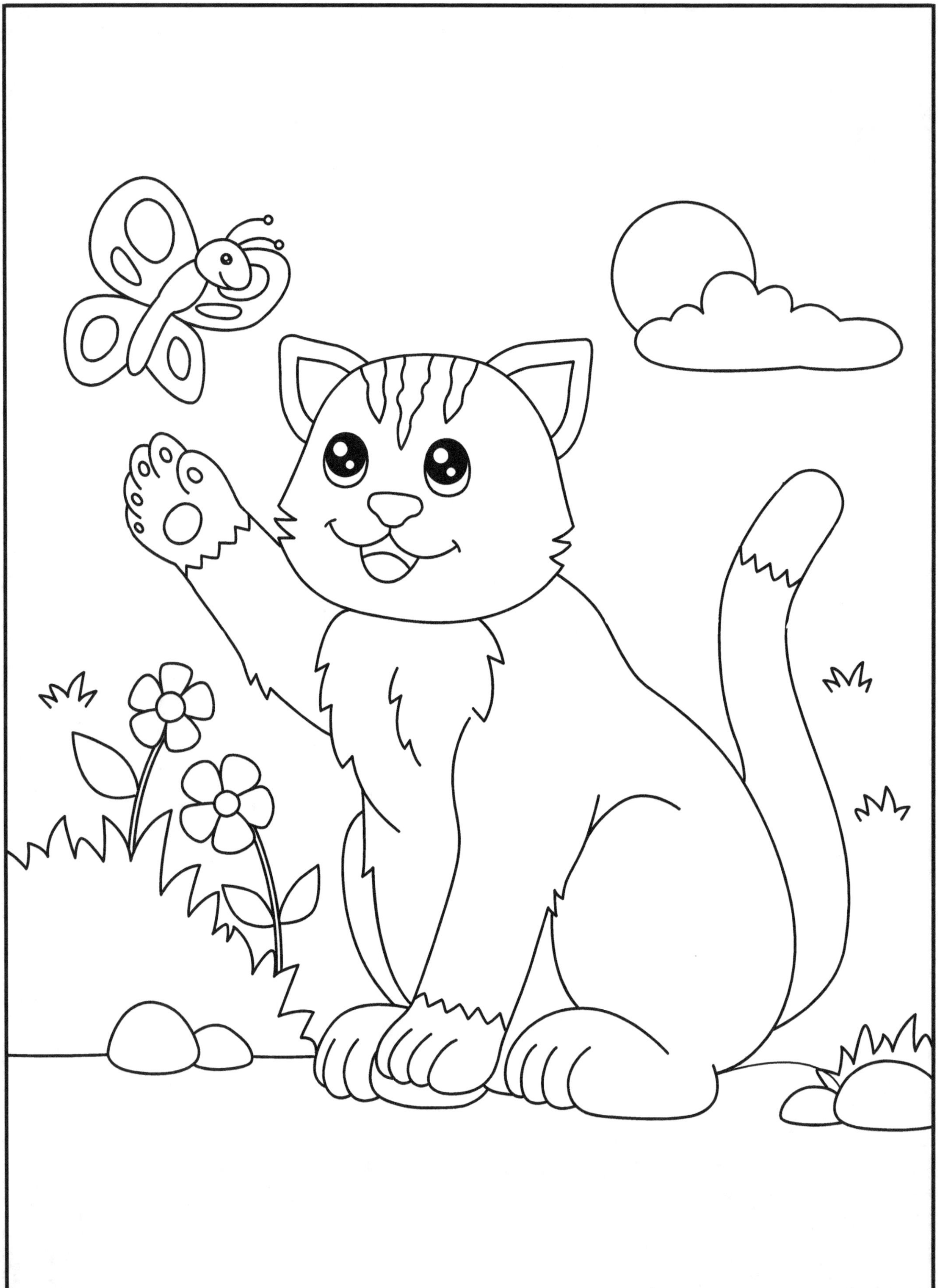

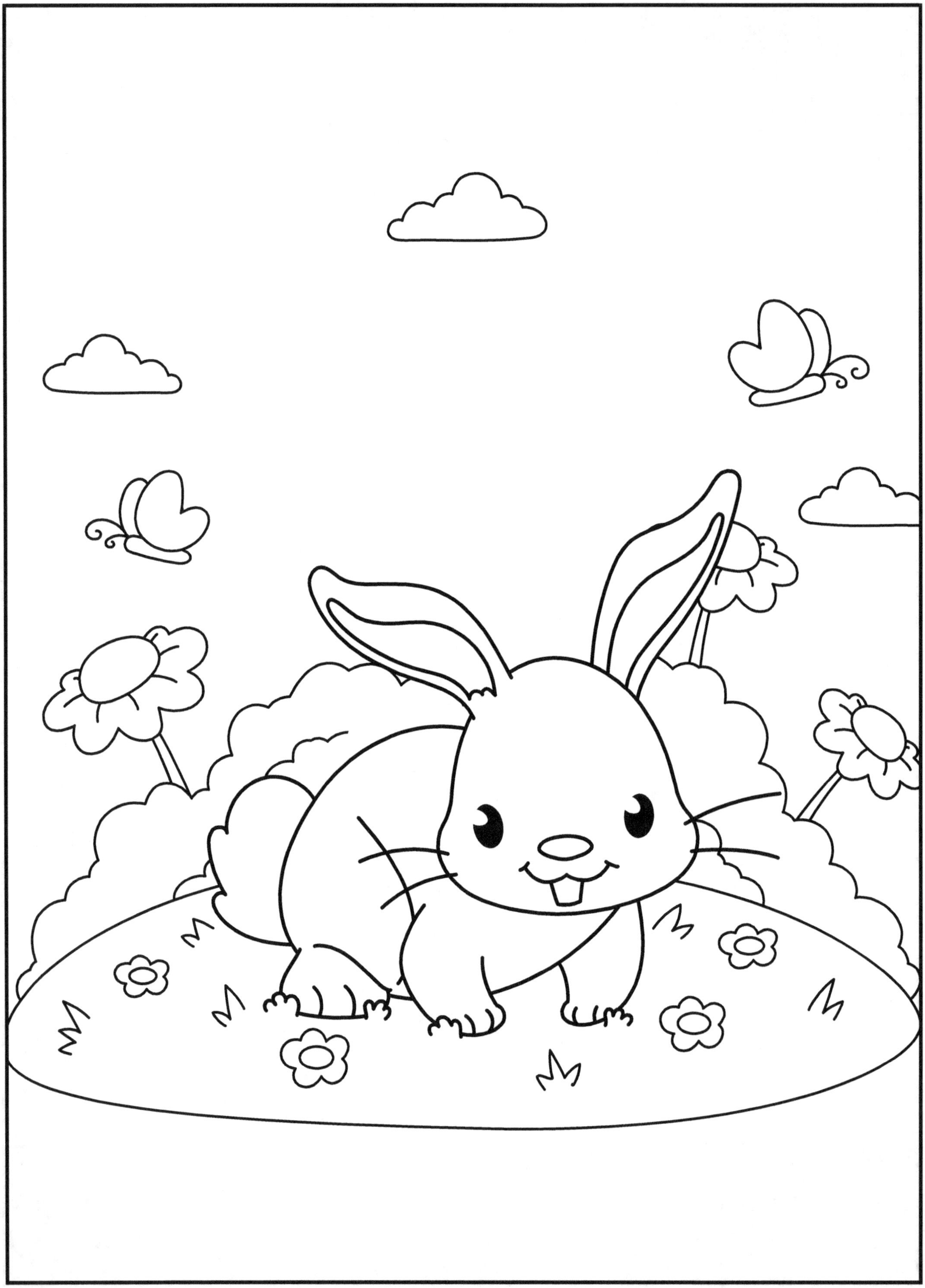

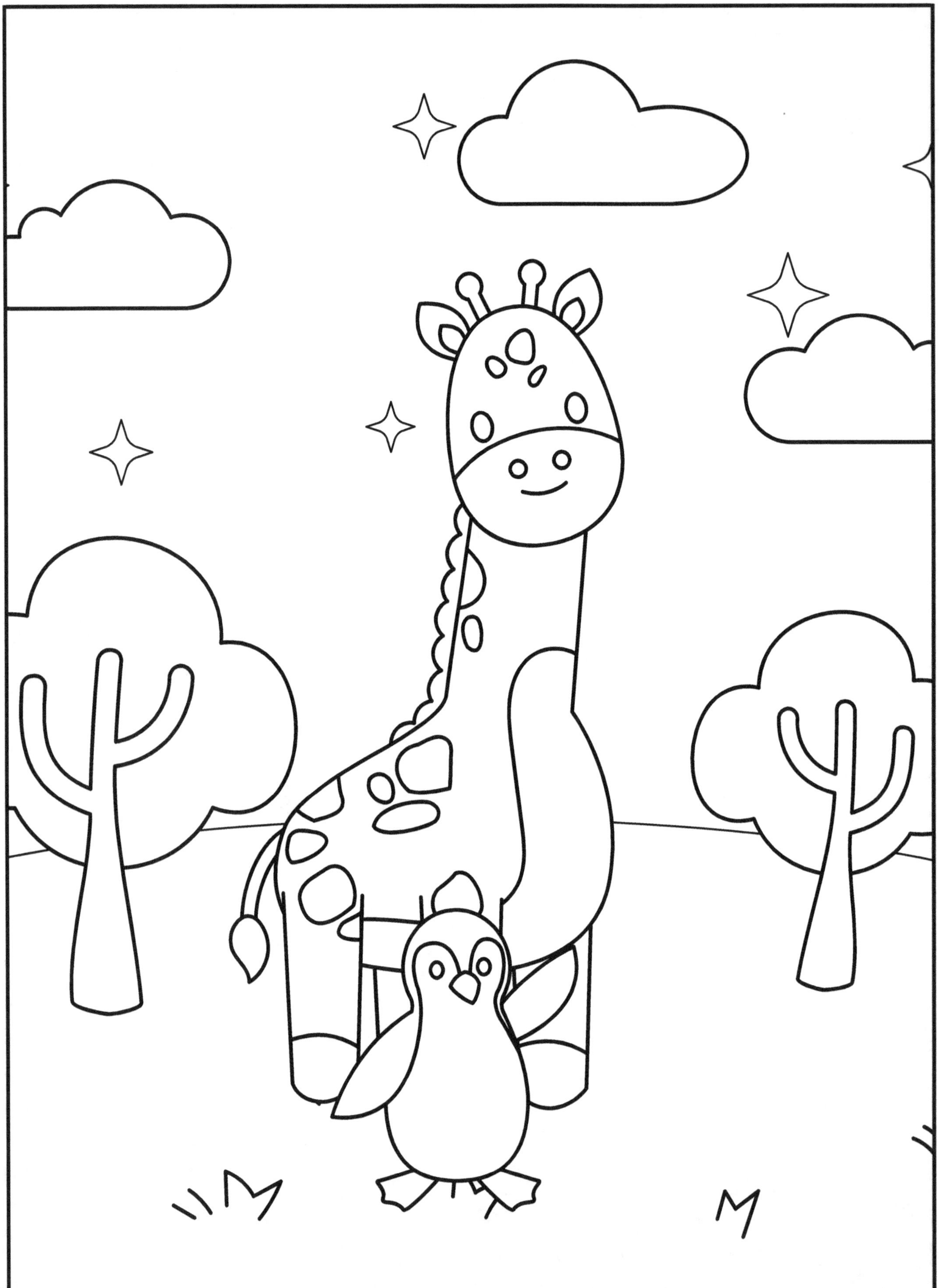

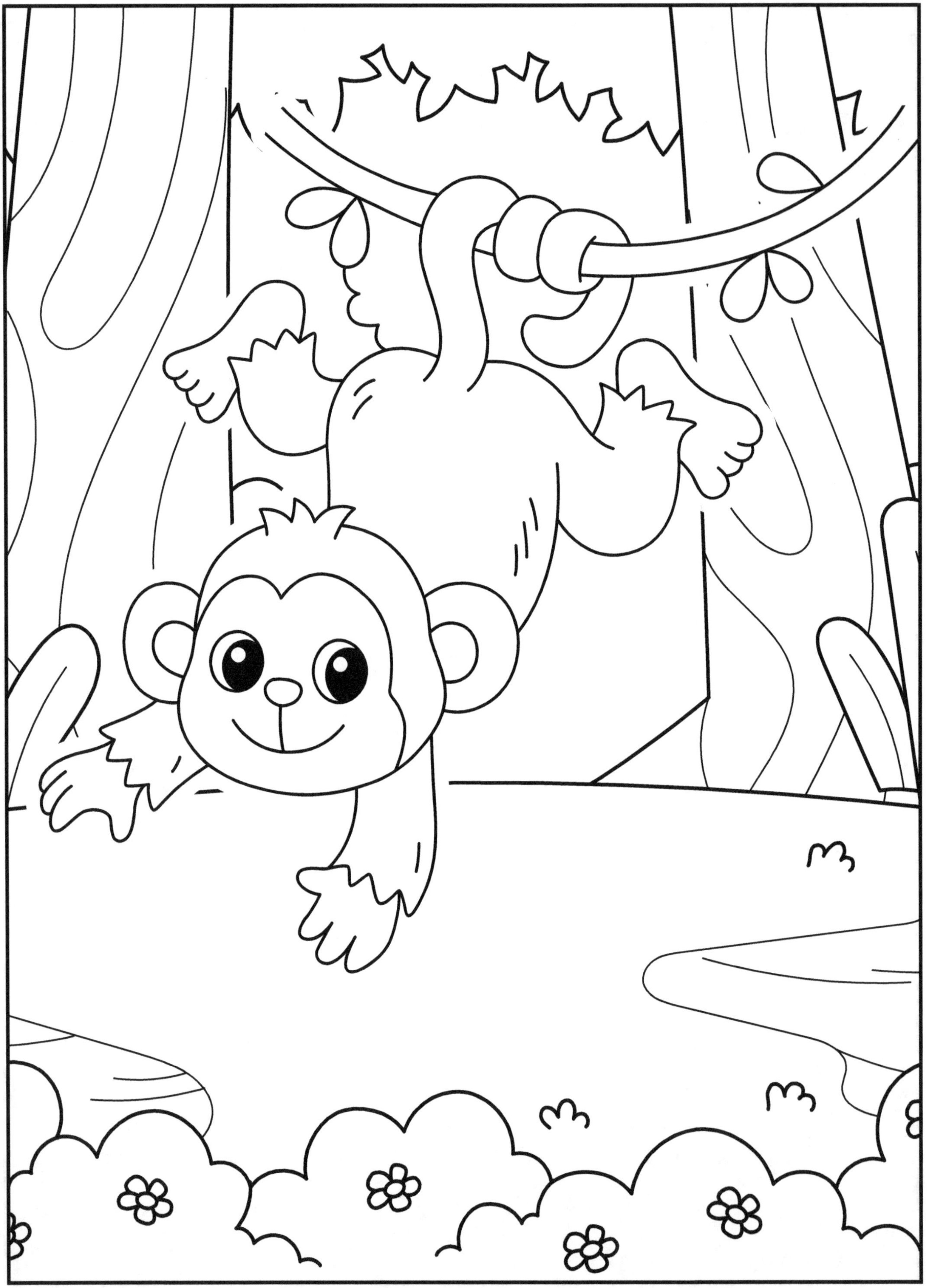

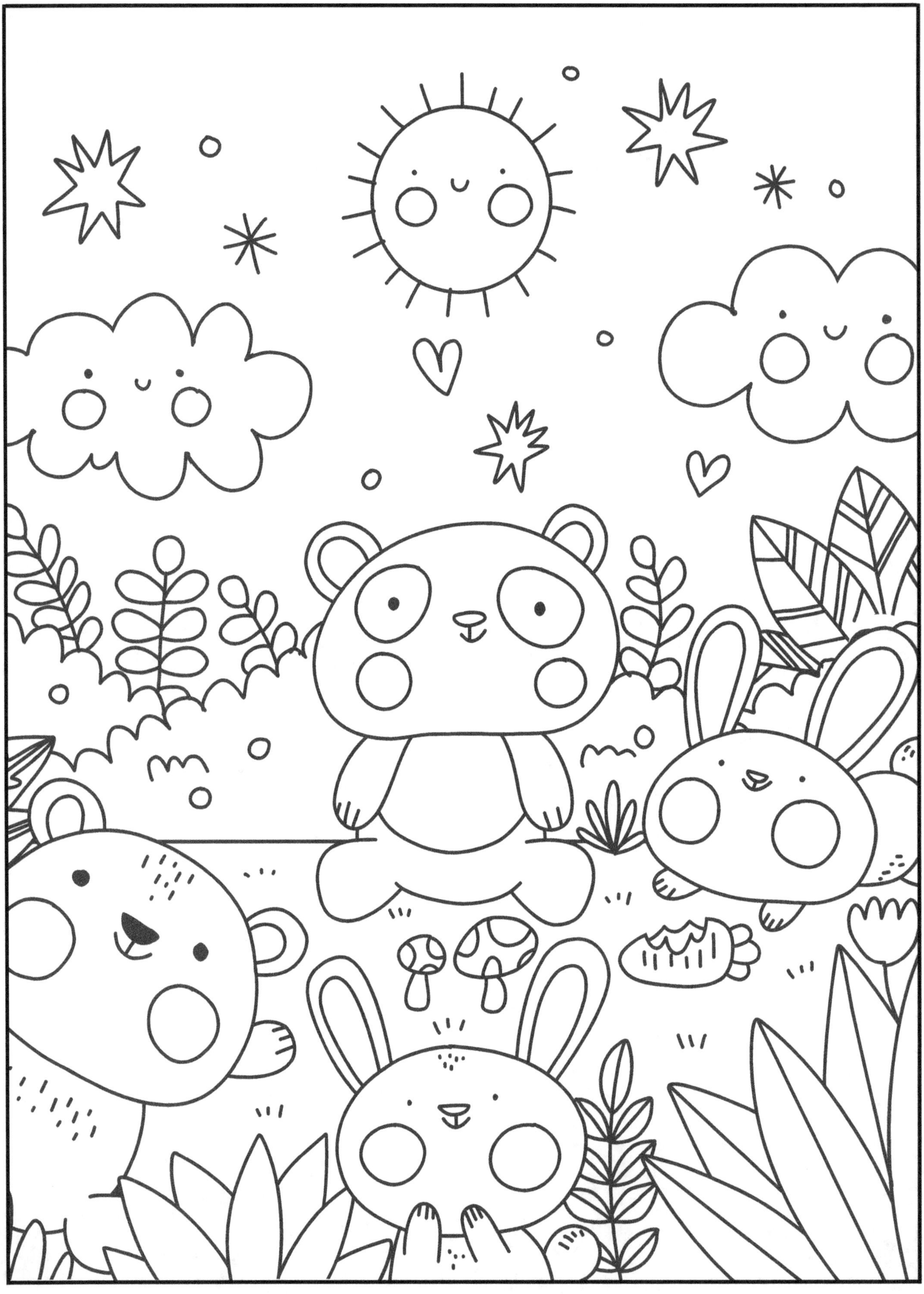

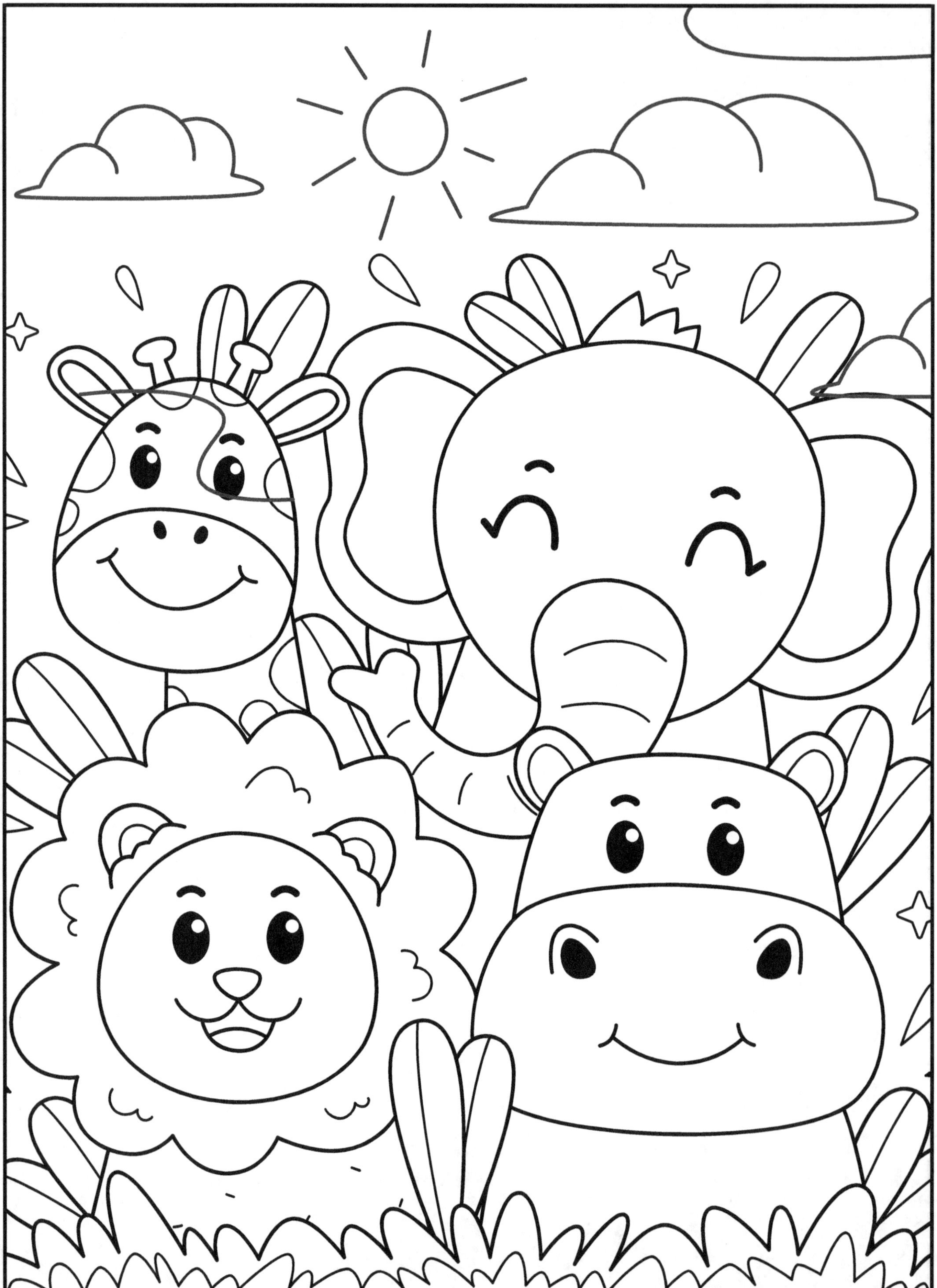

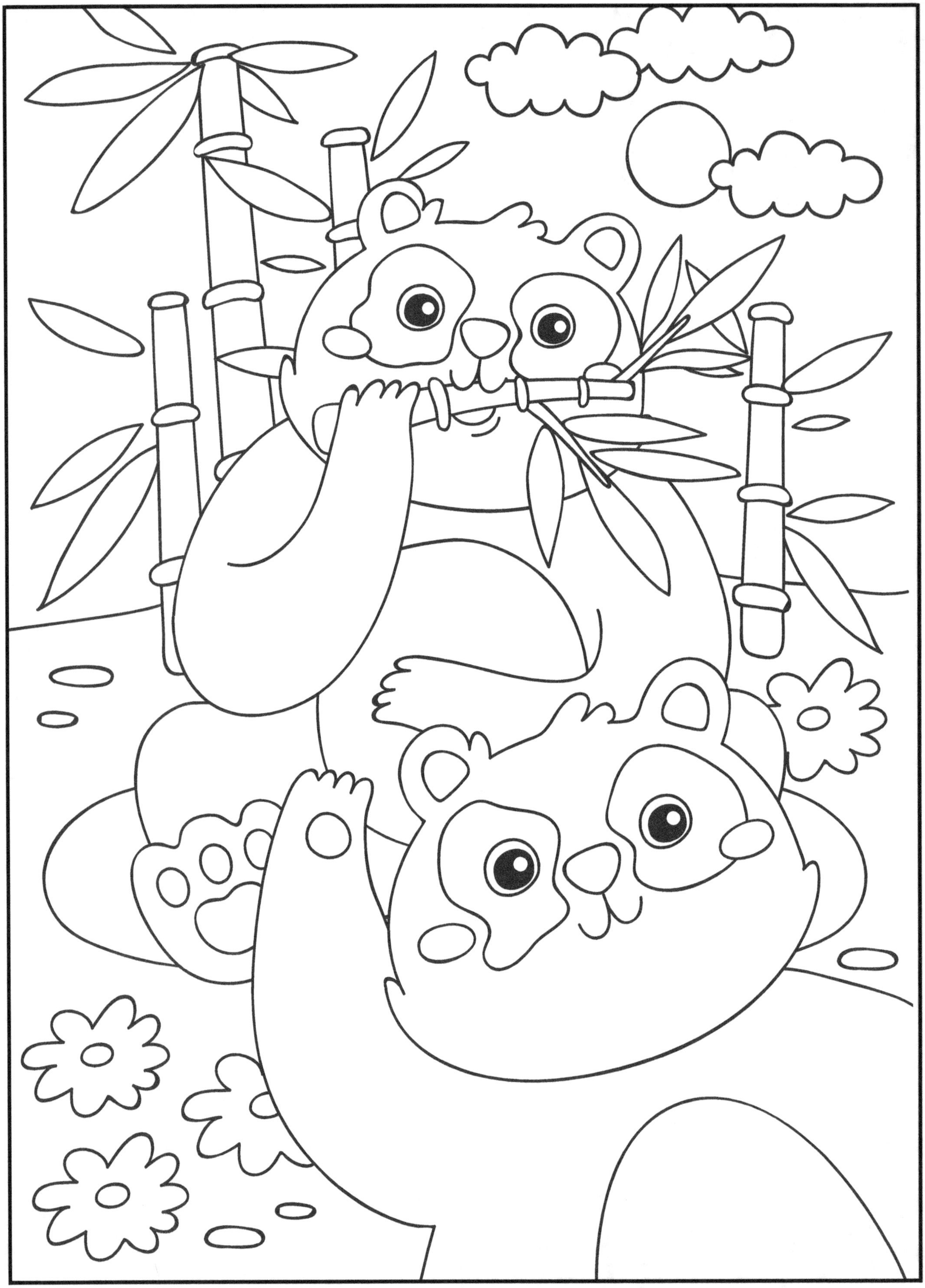

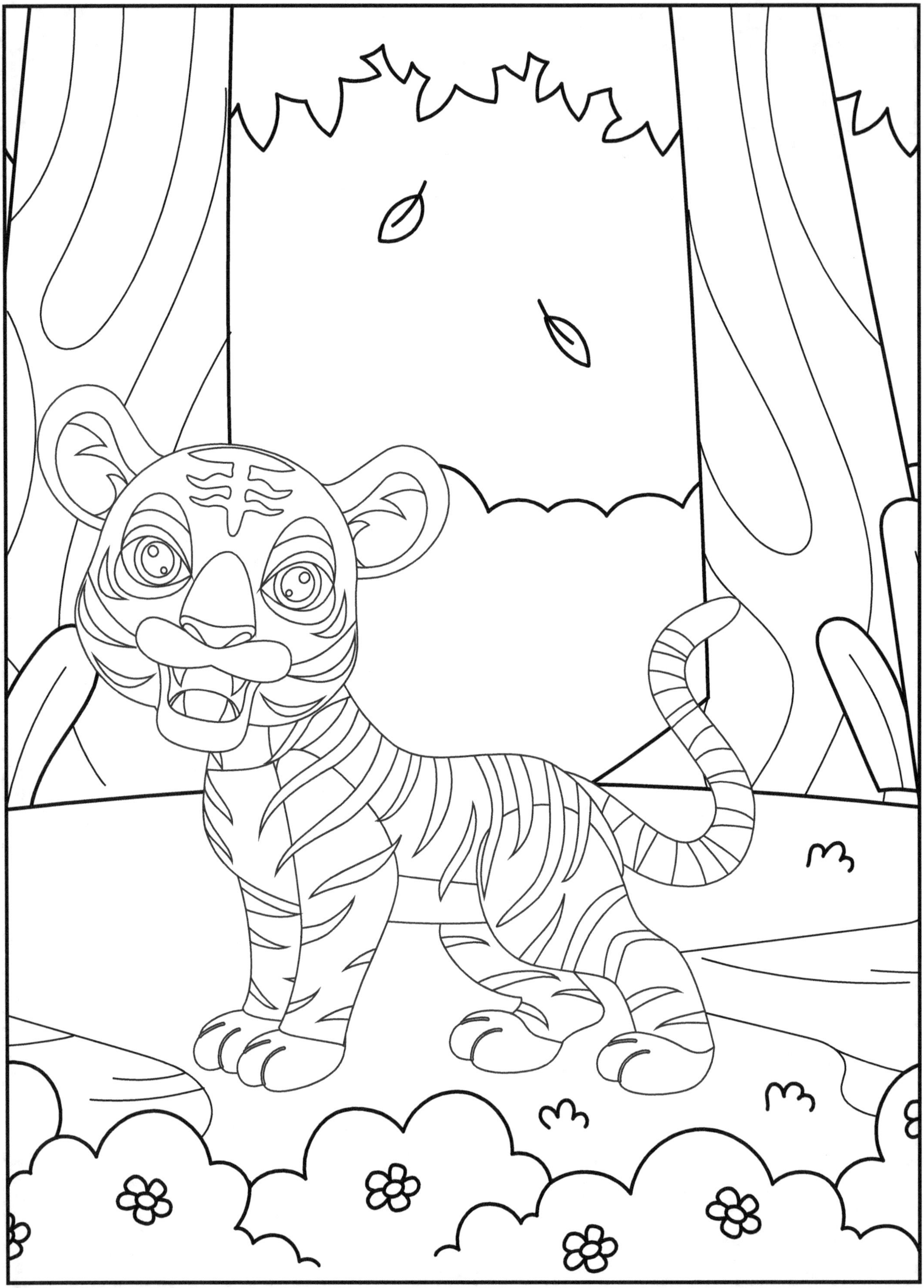

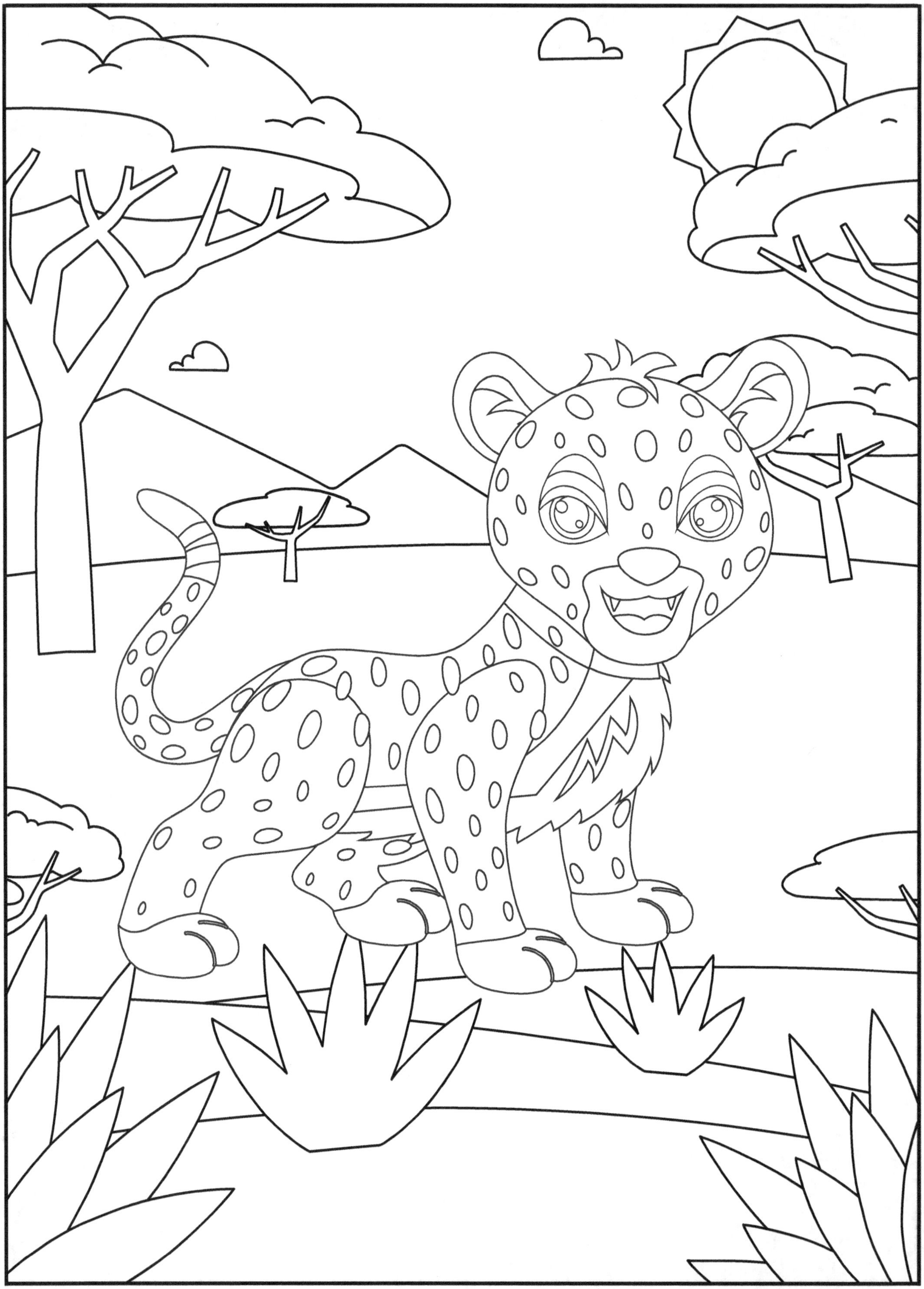

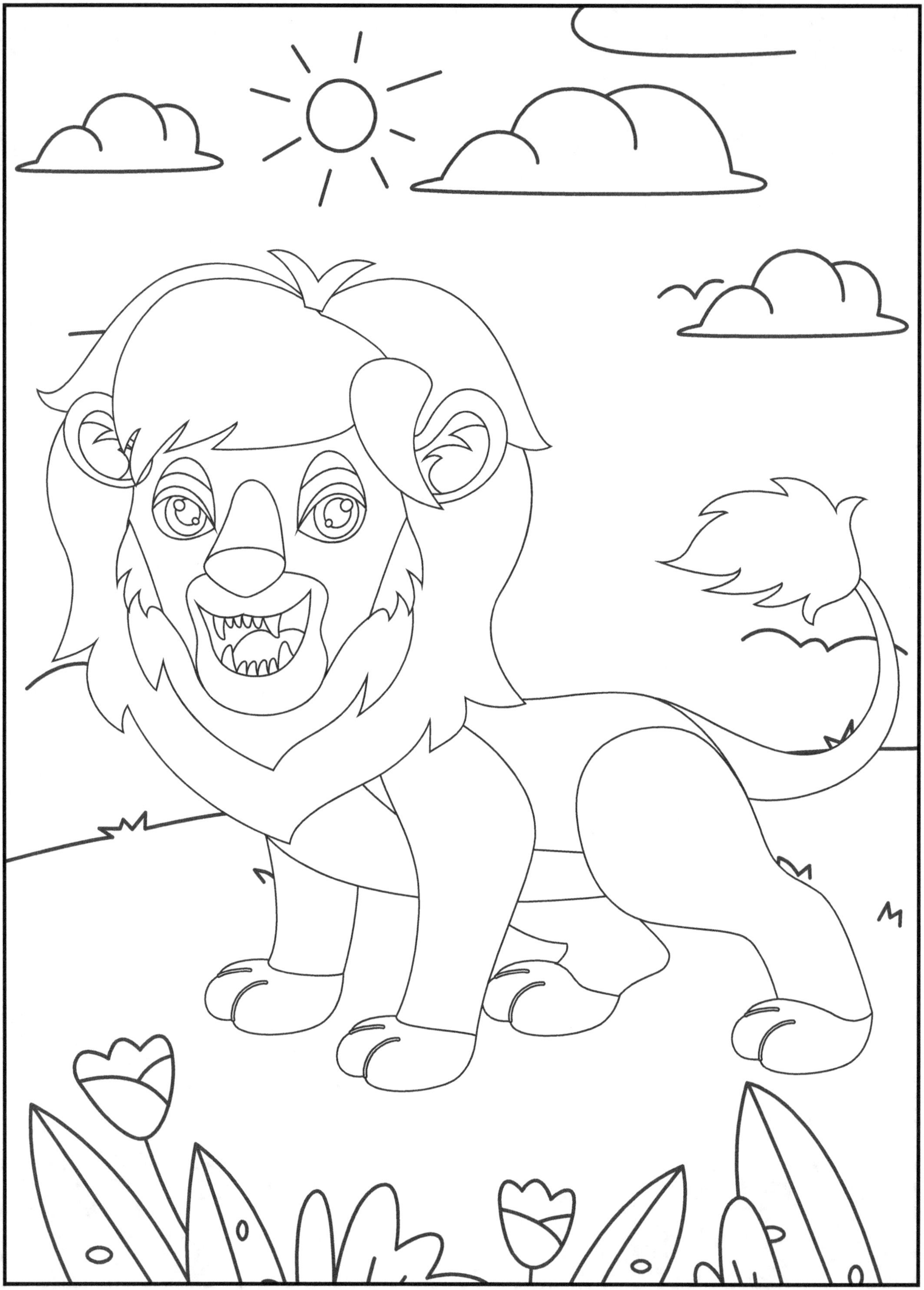

www.ingramcontent.com/pod-product-compliance
Lightning Source LLC
Chambersburg PA
CBHW082208070526
44585CB00020B/2334